the Genesis Cafe

conversations on the kingdom

the Genesis Cafe

conversations on the kingdom

Robby McAlpine

ISBN: 978-0-9881304-4-9

Cover art design and photography by Wendy McAlpine RPP, PPOC

dedication

To my children: Jordan, Caleb, and Renee, who fill my life with love, joy, laughter, and much creative craziness.

This book is for you, and your generation. May the words of the Psalmist also be true of your journey:

"Since my youth, O God, you have taught me, and to this day I declare your marvelous deeds. Even when I am old and gray, do not forsake me, O God, till I declare your power to the next generation, your might to all who are to come." *(Psalm 71:17-18)*

table of contents

the gathering 9

brilliant & broken 27

setting the table 43

salt shaker 59

thor's hammer 79

salsa picante 97

enter jesus 115

storyteller 137

kitchen justice 159

good news 185

coffee & toast 215

about the author 239

acknowledgements

Acknowledgement is simply a fancy way of saying "thank you" to those people who have had a hand in helping shape a writing project. If the word acknowledgement sounds a little stuffy to you, just mentally insert words like kudos, hat-tip, or simply the time-honored *thanks*.

I am grateful for the thoughtful theological critique and suggestions from Jamie Wilson (Pastor @ Coast Vineyard, La Jolla CA), Luke Geraty (Lead Pastor @ Trinity Christian Fellowship, Stanley WI), and my father, Keith McAlpine. Your insights, comments, and 'push-back' were invaluable gifts to me as a writer.

While everyone who reviewed the book had editorial and grammatical input, the formidable skills of Charlotte McAlpine, my mother, were put to the test once again. Thanks, Mom, you've helped make this book readable, and spared me (and my readers) from those grammatical and spelling blunders that spell-check doesn't catch.

My eldest daughter, Jordan McAlpine, provided insightful feedback – along with input from her housemates as she discussed the book with them – and challenged me where I needed to be challenged. You name the area: theology, justice or even my style of writing, and Jordan's passionate input has had an impact somewhere.

The staff and owners of the Lake Country Coffeehouse *(http://lakecountrycoffee.com/)* graciously allowed me to be the 'writer in residence' for the better part of four months during the early drafts of this book. There is no better ambient creative writing zone in the entire Okanagan Valley, and the same goes for their *americanos*.

Wendy McAlpine, my multi-talented and beautiful wife, has once again designed and photographed the cover artwork for this book. It's amazing how she can hear just a few sentences from me about what I'm vaguely picturing in my mind, and then come back with just the right images. And as the first reader of each freshly written chapter, Wendy has also provided ongoing and significant input into the writing.

Finally, to all those who are reading these words: thank you for your interest in my writing, and especially for your interest in the topic of the Kingdom of God. I trust that what you discover in the following pages will challenge and inspire you to love and serve Jesus even more.

And thank you for reading these Acknowledgements. Not everybody does. :)

"This problem must not be solved by abstract theological reasoning but by the exegesis of the Scriptures. The point of departure must always be, 'What do the Scriptures teach?' rather than, 'What does logic allow?' We shall turn therefore to the New Testament, particularly to the teachings of our Lord, for the answer."

George Eldon Ladd, 1952

chapter One
the gathering

It was a near-perfect summer's afternoon, with just the right combination of bright, warm sunlight and a gentle, cooling breeze rustling the leaves of the medium-sized trees lining the boulevard. The timeworn bricks of the early-twentieth-century buildings, so drab and colorless during the cold, wet winter, now cheerfully soaked in and reflected the warm rays of the sun.

After satisfying the unspoken but unmistakable demand of the roadside parking meter for some of my coins, I threaded my way through the bustling pedestrian traffic on the sidewalk, my eyes scanning ahead down the block. There were many cafés to choose from in this busy downtown district, but like most people, I had my own favorite spot in mind.

In one of life's happy coincidences, the traffic light changed just as I arrived at the intersection. Thankful for my good fortune, I joined the crowd briskly striding across the street, the familiar sign over the door of my destination, *The Genesis Café*, beckoning me. Stepping inside, I quickly glanced around the interior, and discovered that, as was often the case, I was the first to arrive.

Spotting a table near the open windows at the front (the one with a great view of the street and blessed by the summer's breeze), I quickly ordered a *café americano* from the barista behind the counter. She was at her usual welcoming and efficient best, which was part of what made the *Genesis* such a great place. The Barista, consciously or not, defied the typical stereotypes: black-clad and multi-pierced, yet cheerful and professional in her work.

I had barely seated myself after claiming the window-side table, when the door burst open again and the two friends I was expecting came noisily inside, already involved in animated conversation. I half-rose from my seat, waving to let them see where I was, and they cheerfully waved in return, en route to the espresso bar. After purchasing their drinks, they joined me with the smiles and greetings of long-time camaraderie.

"I really must apologize for our tardiness," began the Elder, almost before he was seated. "I truly believe the City is gradually *shrinking* the parking spaces on the street, which makes my choices for parking more and more limited as the years go by."

The Younger made a theatrical show of stifling a choking cough. "The problem," he suggested to the Elder, "is that your car is a behemoth-sized land-yacht." Shifting his gaze to me, he added, "I'm starting to think that when 'Leviathan' is mentioned in the book of Job, they were talking about his car."

"I had a car like that once," I sighed, remembering fondly. "A '71 Dodge Monaco, with a 360 cubic inch engine. It was only a two-door, but it was longer than my dad's station wagon. I could fit my entire *life* into the trunk. It was a total rust-bucket, but it was *my* rust-bucket." The Younger laughed in appreciation, although I knew his mind was racing to convert cubic inches to liters. The Elder pretended to be completely fascinated with his coffee as he ignored both of us.

They were an interesting duo, these two friends of mine. The Elder, content in his early retirement, was nonetheless still very much the embodiment of his former occupation as a teacher of classical literature. His fondness for the classics, coupled with his childhood in England (although his accent was barely noticeable these days), had endowed him with a unique and endearing way of expressing himself.

To the surprise of many who made his acquaintance, the Elder had never spent a day in seminary. He was simply an avid reader, and his fascination with learning more about his faith led him to describe himself, in his usual self-deprecating way, as an 'amateur theologian'.

"Remember," he was known to say with a mischievous twinkle, "the original meaning of 'amateur' meant *for the love of it.* Hence my love for learning more about God makes me a truly *amateur* theologian."

The Younger was as restlessly energetic as the Elder was contentedly calm. Still at the beginning of his career, having graduated from university less than a decade earlier, the Younger was also intensely curious about the intersection between faith and everyday life.

For as long as the Younger could remember, the Elder had been a family friend, but as an adult, he had come to appreciate their friendship on an entirely new level. (Not that this prevented the Younger from enjoying some vigorous teasing of his older friend from time to time.)

Their animated conversations about life, spirituality, and justice were a source of enjoyment and challenge that the Younger thrived on.

"Okay, you said you wanted to bounce some ideas around with us. So, here we are. Let's do it," suggested the Younger, abruptly shifting gears and drawing my wandering thoughts back to the present.

Leaning forward, elbows on the table, he unconsciously adopted his signature look of intense curiosity. Very few people possess the unwavering eye contact of the Younger. Or his profound sense of inquisitiveness, for that matter.

The Elder smiled as if he'd just heard a private joke, or perhaps something amusing had occurred to him. "Well, no-one has ever accused us of hiding behind small talk, eh? Even about the era of classic cars."

"Or accused us of subtlety," I replied, saluting them with my *americano*. "That's why I like hanging out with the two of you. Nobody else could put up with us." Taking a brief breath to collect my thoughts, I launched into the topic that captured my attention in recent weeks.

"I've been thinking about writing another book," I began, noting that the Younger's studious expression did not change, while the Elder nodded slightly as if he wasn't altogether surprised. "And, since you guys have always been such a good sounding board, I thought I'd get your input on it."

The Elder raised his eyebrows, as if surprised by my invitation. "I'm more than willing to help in any way that I can," he offered, clasping his hands around his coffee mug. "Although I'm not sure a single conversation would be entirely adequate."

"Which means you'll be buying us a lot of coffee?" suggested the Younger slyly, sensing that an opportunity had presented itself.

"I've been considering what would make the most sense, after writing *Post-Charismatic* a couple of years ago," I continued, addressing the Elder and pretending I hadn't heard the Younger's not-so-subtle suggestion. "I mean, after writing something like that, what would be the most logical subject to follow up with?"

Leaning back in his chair, without breaking eye contact, the Younger became serious again as he wondered aloud, "Is it really all that important that your next book be connected somehow? Couldn't you just write something completely fresh?"

Having already wrestled with that same question, I hastened to clarify. "No, I'm not feeling constrained or putting pressure on myself to do a sequel. And the last thing

I want to do is to get stuck in a rut. But, the longer I thought about it, the more I became convinced about the importance of the *foundations* of our beliefs. What we believe isn't neutral – it can either be healthy, or dysfunctional. For example, if our understanding of the Kingdom of God is skewed, then everything we do based on that skewed assumption will be, for lack of a better word, *skewed*."

"Just don't call it *Post-Skewed* and you'll be fine," quipped the Younger, shifting in his chair, as the breeze from the open window suddenly moved all of our napkins six inches to the right. "Is that the topic you're thinking of? The Kingdom of God?"

"Well, it certainly was central to Jesus' teaching," I responded, as each of us collected our wayward napkins, "and even the gospel that spread during the book of Acts was known as the 'gospel of the Kingdom'. So, I think it's a very foundational question: what did Jesus *mean* when He said 'the Kingdom is near'?"

The Elder looked thoughtful as he sipped his coffee – 'black, the way God drinks it', as he was fond of saying. "What kind of questions do you think need to be asked?" he began, ever mindful of the big picture. "And who is looking for those answers?"

The Younger broke eye contact with me to look at the Elder, as if he were about to say something, thought better of it, and ended by frowning thoughtfully into space. Or perhaps it was the creaky ceiling fan over our table that had captured his attention.

"Well," I began, pausing to take another sip of my *americano*, "part of the larger problem is that a lot of people seem to be throwing around the phrase 'Kingdom of God' these days, but I don't think many of us mean the same thing when we say it. And more importantly, I don't know if many of us are using the term in the way that Jesus used it."

"Ah," replied the Elder, shifting forward in his chair, "so are you planning to focus on the eschatological end-of-the-world aspects, or the present-day stewardship implications, or what exactly?"

"I think I would start by explaining that *eschatological* refers to our beliefs about the future, and humanity's destiny," I suggested with a laugh.

The Younger's gaze refocused itself from space – or the ceiling fan – and settled again on the Elder. "Hang on a second, professor. Can you really separate them," he asked doubtfully, "without missing something important?"

The Elder surreptitiously moved his coffee mug beyond the reach of his young friend's animated hand gestures, smiling at the Younger's familiar nickname for him.

"That's precisely the question I was about to ask," he replied. "There are so many emphases on different aspects of the Kingdom going around these days, that it would be tempting to only deal with one of them.

"And that, in my opinion, would be a disservice to the totality of what Jesus meant."

"That's probably the most daunting thing in this writing project," I admitted, taking the opportunity to finish the remainder of my *americano*. "The Kingdom of God is a massive topic, on so many levels. I don't want to gloss over anything, but at the same time, I need to have a fairly tight focus to keep it from getting too long."

"What's the title going to be?" asked the Younger, almost interrupting in his eagerness.

Taken aback slightly, I had to admit that I hadn't thought that far in advance. "I'm assuming that a title will make itself known as the material is created," I replied with a shrug. "Choosing a title is usually one of the last things for me, when I write."

The Elder frowned thoughtfully, before adding, "At the same time, a title could serve as a thesis statement, which can help you sharpen your focus." I nodded in agreement, seeing the merit in his suggestion, although I didn't want to get hung up on the title before even beginning the writing.

"It's about the Kingdom, stupid!" exclaimed the Younger loudly, slapping his hand on the table for emphasis. The condiments on the table, gathered in their usual formation next to the wall under the open window, rattled in protest.

The Elder attempted to mollify him. "Yes, obviously it's about the Kingdom. We just said that. I see no reason to be insulting."

"No, no, no," the Younger disagreed amiably, becoming more animated by the minute. "I meant that's what the *title* should be: 'It's About The Kingdom, Stupid!' When I was in university, I remember learning about a politician who campaigned successfully on the slogan: 'it's the economy, stupid'. It was his way of stating what the important issues really were. So, for your book, this title would be a great way to let people know, right from the beginning, that the Kingdom of God is the basis for everything."

I had to laugh. "Yes, that would be a very direct, in-your-face way of summing up the book. And for the record, I *do* plan on emphasizing that the Kingdom of God is our foundation. *That's* why we need to make sure we understand what Jesus really meant when He spoke about the Kingdom. But as the title of the book? Sorry, but I'm not convinced."

The Elder nodded vigorously. "You would do well to avoid the appearance of insulting the intelligence of people who haven't read anything beyond the front cover. Not everyone will recognize or understand the historical reference to an old politician."

"And you should never mix politics and religion, I know, I know," the Younger conceded with a chuckle, although you could tell that his enthusiasm for the title suggestion had barely subsided. "But still, you never know... people might pick it up out of curiosity *because* they thought it was offensive!"

I wished that I still had some of my *americano* left to drink, if only to buy a little time as I considered how to respond. Out of the corner of my eye, I could see the Elder intently studying the slight quivers of coffee in his mug, and I realized he was trying to stifle laughter.

At last, he simply took a deep breath and remarked, "*This* is what happens when you have several voices speaking into the same situation." The Younger looked as if he were about to defend his suggestion once more, but I took advantage of the turn of events to voice the request that I'd come prepared with.

"And that's why I wanted to talk to both of you," I quickly interjected, looking back and forth at each of them. "I don't want to be the only voice in this. I'd like the two of you to be a part of telling this story."

Both of them were looking intently at me by this time, expressionless. "I'm inviting the two of you to be a part of writing this book."

The two of them glanced at each other, the Elder with raised eyebrows, and the Younger uncharacteristically waiting to see what his long-time friend would say first, before committing himself. Before either of them could disagree, I pushed on.

"You both have an interesting take on things," I continued, leaning on the table, which shifted slightly on the uneven flooring.

"When I listen to your conversations, I hear two voices expressing concepts in a way that anyone can understand and relate to. And if I'm totally honest," I admitted, somewhat sheepishly, "I can come across as a little too theologically verbose at times."

"I didn't say that," protested the Younger, holding up his hands in mock surrender, but making no attempt to disguise a wide grin.

Before I could respond, the Elder spoke up. "Well, if you think a couple of rabble-rousers like us could be of service, then by all means, I'd be happy to assist you any way I can."

"Count me in," the Younger chimed in immediately, serious but still grinning.

Leaning forward across the table, folding his hands in front of him, the Elder was suddenly all business. "Who is your target audience? And getting back to my earlier query, what questions do you think most need answering?"

Thankful for the Elder's practical bent, I replied, "I'm hoping to write something that will be accessible to the average layperson who is interested in knowing more about the Kingdom of God, that doesn't require a degree in theology first."

"As far as which questions need answering," I paused for a deep breath, "I'd want to start with what Jesus meant when He preached 'the gospel of the kingdom', and how the early disciples understood and spread that message after Jesus left."

"Absolutely *crucial,*" concurred the Elder, nodding emphatically. "Jesus didn't begin to mention His crucifixion to the disciples until much later in His earthly ministry, which begs the question of what the 'gospel of the kingdom' that He taught at the beginning actually meant."

"Don't forget the justice issues," the Younger insisted. "There has to be a practical dimension to the Kingdom in the here and now. Jesus had a *lot* to say about ethics."

I nodded in agreement, "And the ethical/justice issues are as much personal as they are communal. In other words, what are the personal *and* corporate implications of being 'in the Kingdom'?"

"And what constitutes participation in the Kingdom?" added the Elder, finishing his coffee and replacing his mug on the wooden tabletop. "And let's not forget, *how* and *when* does the Kingdom come?"

As we looked back and forth at each other, all three of us began to laugh. It was a good moment – the realization that we were all excited about diving into the topic as a little community of friends.

As the moment passed, I suggested, "I'll start putting together a framework for the book, and you two can, well, just do what you do best: have a couple of pints and talk."

The Younger and Elder exchanged conspiratorial looks, yet neither seemed able to come up with a suitable retort.

As the after-work crowd began to line up at the counter, we stood to make our table available, gathering our coffee mugs together and depositing them into the bin next to the espresso counter.

The Elder again became quite serious as he asked, "I assume you'll be referencing the work of Ladd on this topic, am I right?"

The Younger looked puzzled, but I answered the Elder, "Of course. The 'already and not yet' Kingdom of God. Ladd's writings on the Kingdom are brilliant."

The Elder turned to the Younger, noticing his friend's perplexed silence. "Are we dating ourselves – revealing our advanced age? Have you heard of George Eldon Ladd? Or his influential book: *Jesus and the Kingdom*?"

The Younger just shook his head, holding his hands out in a gesture of helplessness.

"It's actually been re-titled *The Presence of the Future*, in recent years," I amended, although I could see that the Younger appeared as unenlightened as before.

This confirmed something that had been percolating in the back of my mind for some time, and now seemed as good a time as any to mention it. "Perhaps it's time to re-introduce Ladd's writings on the Kingdom to the next generation," I said, addressing the Elder. "We tend to assume that everyone is familiar with Ladd and his work on the Kingdom because he is quoted by so many other authors, but I'm meeting a lot of younger people who have never heard of Ladd or his books."

"You can include me on that list," agreed the Younger, with a self-deprecating shrug. "I've never heard of him, but it sounds like that's all about to change." Holding the door open, he gestured us through. "Allow me to show respect to the *older* generation."

"Psalm 71:18: 'Till I declare your power to the next generation, your might to all who are to come,'" quoted the

Elder, as he led the way outside. "Although I hesitate to place myself in the role of the Psalmist, who described himself as 'old and grey'."

"But with the wisdom of Solomon," I hastened to add, schooling myself to keep a straight face, and pretending not to notice the Younger's barely-stifled guffaw. "Why don't we each invest some time reading through *The Presence of the Future* before we meet again, as the starting point for our conversations?"

The Elder nodded as he adjusted his cap. "Yes, I'll dig out my old, *original title* copy, and the two of us will put our heads together. And perhaps a copy of the newer edition needs to be purchased by the young and uninitiated among us."

The Younger looked momentarily offended, but then nodded sheepishly in agreement. "I'll get my own copy. I like to make notes and comments in the margins, and I know how much it drives him crazy when other people write in his books," he said, jerking his thumb in the Elder's direction. The Elder merely tipped his hat in reply.

And with a few warm farewells, we parted ways, the two of them setting off in the opposite direction from where I'd parked earlier.

The afternoon sun had moved on, allowing long shadows to overtake the interlocking brick sidewalks, but the trees still sighed and rustled in the cool breeze. I was pleased to see that there was still time remaining on the parking meter as I returned to my car. And as I settled behind the steering wheel, probing with my key for the ignition, I recognized the familiar feeling of anticipation, discovery, and excitement that accompanies the first steps in writing a book.

And I sensed, as the engine came to life and I signaled my turn into traffic, that our journey into understanding what Jesus meant when He said 'the Kingdom is near' was going to be *life changing*.

Further Conversations

Note: while you can easily benefit from these questions individually, there's nothing quite like discussing things with good friends over coffee, pints, or even french fries. Call it a small group, or a book club, or whatever you want. The book is written as a conversation between friends; why not do the same?

Just sayin'.

1. Where is your 'third place'? If you were to go somewhere to have a discussion with friends where would you go? What makes it your favorite?
2. To which of the characters do you relate most easily? Most of us have people like this in our lives: a peer with whom you can discuss things, an elder that you look up to for perspective and wisdom, and someone who is both learning from and challenging you. Who are these people in your life?

   If they include some of the people in your group, stop here and tell each other what you appreciate and value about each other.
3. The main points of theology are introduced in the conversation between the three characters. Make a topic list with your own questions about each point. "Theology" simply means the *study of God*. That makes everyone who thinks about what they believe about God a theologian (congrats!), so don't be intimidated by the word or the idea.

4. Agree/Disagree: Theological ideas need to be interpreted by our culture to make sense.

Tip: Have a Bible handy while reading this book. Check out the different verses that are quoted, and that the author is using the Bible responsibly.

chapter Two

brilliant & broken

A couple of days after recruiting the Younger and Elder at the *Genesis*, I managed to find a few uninterrupted hours in the late afternoon and sought out a quiet spot in a park downtown, not far from the lake's edge. From here, one can marvel at the beauty of the mountains on the far side of the lake (the entire town is built around and on the mountainsides) or you can, as I intended on this sunny afternoon, bury yourself in a book.

Even before the Elder suggested that we explore George Eldon Ladd's written works on the Kingdom of God, I had been planning to immerse myself in Ladd's books. It was true, as the Elder had pointed out, that many of those who have written on the topic of the Kingdom all refer to Ladd's writings as an influence.

I had enjoyed and been thoroughly challenged when I read *The Presence of the Future*, the book which Ladd had invested ten years of his life in researching and writing.

(The Elder owned an older copy, when it was still known by its original title, *Jesus and the Kingdom*).

The book was nothing short of exhaustively brilliant. It took me longer than usual to finish it. The book was inspiring, and I often found myself pausing as I read, to let the implications of what I was reading sink in. On the other hand, theologically speaking, the book was challenging due to its depth, which often caused me to pause as well (if only to give my head a shake). I came away impressed by Ladd's scholarship, and inspired by the message of the Kingdom of God in his book.

But today was different, as I wandered along the pathway in the park, looking for just the right location. I had brought with me a copy of a recently published biography about Ladd, entitled *A Place at the Table*. I had already read it, the day before our meeting at the *Genesis Café*, and I wanted to carve out some time to reflect on Ladd's life, his work, and the impact of both sides of that story: the man himself, and the incredible legacy he left in his books, and those whom he had influenced.

George Eldon Ladd was a fascinating character, although writing a glowing script for an inspirational Christian movie about his life would prove challenging. His impact on how we view the Kingdom is immense, and for that, he is easy to hold in high esteem. His personal life, on the other hand, was something of a continual train-wreck-in-progress, which I had found both sad and disturbing. *The Younger would probably describe Ladd's life as 'really messed up'*, I thought.

Still, when I considered the biblical lessons we can learn from the flawed lives of Old Testament characters such as Samson, I felt challenged to learn from all of Ladd's life, including the less-than-praiseworthy parts.

Already lost in thought, I jolted back to the present and found myself near a park bench perfectly tucked under the shade of a weeping willow tree, just a few meters away from the water. I sat down on the bench, gazing at the rippling waves and hearing the rustling of the willow as the westerly breeze stirred its branches. The perfect setting for a little reading, relaxation, and reflection.

The bare facts of Ladd's early life, while only part of the story, provide an important context for his later life and ministry. George Eldon Ladd was born in 1911, and grew up in an impoverished home. Ladd became a Christian in a Methodist church, and his years of ministry, both pastoral and as a seminary professor, were a testimony to the grace of God and the frailty of humanity.

Ladd's childhood was marked by poverty, but more so by a dysfunctional relationship with his parents, especially his father, which continued to affect him throughout his life. Ladd's brother was the 'golden child' favored by his father, and Ladd grew up always feeling inadequate and ignored. Perhaps not surprisingly, he developed a huge need for recognition and validation, which would lead him into all kinds of trouble, even as he was emerging as one of the foremost thinkers and writers in his field.

What made Ladd unique among his peers was that he remained firmly evangelical in his faith, while at the same time, he engaged in dialogue with the 'liberal' interpretations of the Bible that dominated 'serious' scholarship in his day. Unafraid to use the tools of the 'liberal' academy, Ladd graduated with his Doctorate from Harvard and yet never flinched in his evangelical faith.

It was an era when many Christians, after being humiliated in the evolution-versus-creation "Scopes Monkey Trial" (a literal trial, in a courthouse in Tennessee), had chosen to retreat from the public arena, and had begun to create their own Christian subcultures. In stark contrast to this retreat, Ladd was determined to prove that evangelical Christians could compete intellectually and within the academy of higher learning. It was a bold and demanding goal, and Ladd invested himself in its pursuit, heart and soul.

Breaking my gaze from the mesmerizing effect of the waves, I quickly skimmed through a few sections that I'd highlighted in the biography. Even though I am well aware that none of us are perfect, it was still hard to believe how tragic this incredibly wise and learned man's life had been.

Ladd's marriage to Winnie, a woman who came from as broken and dysfunctional a family as his own, was difficult, to say the least. This awkward relationship, compounded by his obsession with his work, resulted in him neglecting his family. The fruit of this choice was evident later in an embittered daughter and a neglected (and later alcoholic) son. Near the end of his life, Ladd struggled with depression and developed a drinking problem, which eventually escalated into full-blown alcoholism.

Despite the difficulties in their marriage, Winnie's death, just one year after his retirement, seemed to cause Ladd a great deal of guilt and pain. After her death, Ladd fell further into depression, and an increased dependency on alcohol. This tailspin would continue until his death in 1982 at the age of seventy-one.

Somewhere in the distance, my brain registered the harsh cries of squabbling seagulls, fighting over a garbage can further down the walkway. Looking up from the book, I admired again the mountains rising out of the deep blue expanse before me, as I thought about what I'd read. Ladd's life story was already becoming something of a 'living parable', as I considered how such a tragic and broken person could be so powerfully used by God. And yet, the warning side of the parable was impossible to ignore.

Ladd wrote convincingly on the present reality of the Kingdom of God, and thoroughly refuted the dominant evangelical mind-set of the time: dispensationalism, which taught (among other things) that the Kingdom was entirely in the future, and therefore teachings like the Sermon on the Mount didn't apply to Christians today. The belief that there is no point in taking care of the environment because "it's all going to burn anyway" can trace its roots directly to dispensationalism.

(I could almost hear the Younger's voice in my head, protesting the mere existence of a term like *dispensationalism*. "If they're trying to describe different periods in history, why not just say that? Or choose a metaphor that makes sense, like: 'history is divided into different chapters, like a book'. Inventing a new term just makes it confusing for us normal people.")

During his years as a professor, Ladd authored a scholarly volume of work, the apex of which was *Jesus and the Kingdom.* Many scholars, in Ladd's day as well as ours, applauded and embraced his view of the "already and not yet" nature of the Kingdom of God. (I smiled to myself, anticipating how much fun the Younger and the Elder would have as they unpacked what that meant.)

But one of the most prominent liberal scholars of the day, Norman Perrin from the University of Chicago, wrote a scathing review and rebuttal to *Jesus and the Kingdom.* That single negative review devastated Ladd, convincing him that his life's mission of raising the level of evangelical scholarship had been a complete and abject failure. Ladd had already been struggling with alcohol abuse, and the depression that set in after Perrin's pointed refutation precipitated a downward spiral into greater alcoholism.

The seagulls settled their argument at last, or perhaps their screaming in-air progress across the lake signified a bird-mob pursuit for whatever morsel had so completely captured their attention.

I was looking forward to the three of us – the Younger, the Elder, and I – delving into Ladd's writing in greater detail as we discussed the Kingdom of God. But from the outset, I also recognized that there were some very important life lessons staring back at me from the pages of Ladd's biography.

I set aside the hardcover book, and picked up my journal, protected as always with the Levi's denim cover that a friend had given me years earlier. As the sound of the seagull mob diminished west and north, I scanned the notes from my first reading, and began to scribble my thoughts into the journal balanced on my knee.

1. Where do I find my identity?

Most of us would naturally respond, "Why, my identity is found in Christ Jesus, of course". Trouble is, I suspect Ladd would have said the same thing, most likely for the same reasons. And we'd be telling the truth. Or at least, giving the "correct answer" that we knew we were expected to believe.

But when our sense of identity is hit hard by criticism, failure (real or perceived), or any number of disappointments in life, it's not unusual for our head knowledge about our identity in Christ to be nearly drowned out by the screaming insecurities in our hearts.

If we measure our sense of identity in what we do, and even more so when we base our identity on people's *approval* of what we do, we are setting ourselves up for wounding and disillusionment.

On two occasions (that were recorded), Jesus heard the audible affirmation of His Father: "This is my Son, whom I love; with him I am well pleased." The first was at Jesus' baptism, at the beginning of His public ministry (Mark 1:10-11, Luke 3:21-22). The second was at His

Transfiguration, just before the events leading up to His death by crucifixion (Matthew 17:5, Mark 9:7-8).

What kind of impact does knowing that we are 'sons' and 'daughters' of God have on me? Is having God's approval enough?

2. Whose approval is the most important to me?

Ladd had many positive voices in his life, thanking him and applauding his scholarly efforts. These voices should have created a deep sense of gratitude that he was truly making a difference in the lives of others.

There were also the negative voices of those who disagreed or openly opposed him, yet you would think that the good voices would at least balance out the negative. But it seemed that the positive comments were somehow disqualified, because the people that Ladd really wanted to hear affirmation from either ignored or actually opposed his best efforts.

I know where I've been guilty of that, I thought to myself, *in my musical hopes and dreams*. Like most musicians (or artistic types in general), there were certain 'heroes' that I looked up to, and gaining their approval could easily become a neurotic obsession. Honest compliments from others were encouraging, yes, but what I really wanted was for 'serious' musicians to consider me capable of playing on their level. And if that didn't happen, the temptation awaiting me was to respond as Ladd did: "There's no point. I give up."

I looked up at the mountains across the lake, sobered by the realization that the same could be true for any book that I may write, as well. For that matter, any number of other areas in my life could also be susceptible. Whose approval was the most important? And what would my reaction be if I didn't receive it? Despair? Disillusionment?

Or potentially more damning, what kind of person would I become if I *did* receive their affirmation? Prideful? Elitist? Filled with selfish ambition?

Jesus taught that "sharing the joy of (our) Master" went hand-in-hand with hearing the words "well done, good and faithful servant" (Matthew 25:21). Are these words of approval from Jesus truly the most important for me?

3. Where do I turn when things go sideways?

Ladd had a tendency to be a workaholic at the best of times, but the criticism that wounded him resulted in his withdrawal even further into his work, and later into abusing alcohol. There are countless stories of people whose lives have spiraled into addictions of some kind when their life got out of control, whether through positive or negative circumstances. Sudden success can be as deadly as sudden failure.

An ache in my right hand distracted me momentarily, causing me to stop writing so I could shake out the cramp that had bitten deeply into the muscle between my thumb and forefinger.

3b. Where do I turn for comfort?

Too few of us, myself included, follow the example of King David and many others in the Bible. How many times do we see the phrase "pour out my soul" or something similar in the Old Testament? How many times did the Israelites "cry out to God" for relief?

There are many examples of this to be found throughout the Bible. In one of Peter's epistles, we are actually *instructed* to pour out our cares, concerns, and frustrations to Jesus (I Peter 5:6-7). Again, this is the 'correct answer', something that would earn me a gold star in Sunday School when I was young. But when it really matters, do I run to God with my cares, my concerns, my fears, and my failures?

Is "casting my cares" on Jesus truly enough for me?

4. Relationship. Relationship. Relationship.

Ladd was so focused, so driven, so consumed with his 'mission' in life, that he neglected his wife and children, and it had a devastating effect on all of them. And as the relational distance between them increased, Ladd withdrew even further, burying himself in his work. When his wife died after a long illness, Ladd was in a different city on a speaking engagement.

It reminded me of a *Star Trek: Deep Space Nine* re-run I'd seen recently, where the ship's captain admonished his son, who is obsessed with writing his first novel: "Poke your head up every once in a while. Take a look around.

See what's going on. It's *life*, and you can miss it, if you don't open your eyes."

We get one chance to be newlyweds. To be new parents. To run beside a five-year-old, as she wobbles on her bicycle, without training wheels for the first time. To put the Flintstones Band-Aid on the boy's knee and 'kiss it all better'. To sit on a cold metal bleacher and cheer together for the local football team. To celebrate another anniversary over a candle-lit dinner.

The sobering lesson from Ladd's family life is painfully clear: some things are more important than our 'life's mission'. Our marriage, our children, our extended families, and our friendship circles. As my wife Wendy has observed, "If we win the whole city to Jesus, but lose our own children in the process, we've failed in the most important ministry God called us to."

My hand began to cramp up again, requiring me to set my pen aside, as I massaged the ache with my other hand. As I worked to relax my writing hand, I glanced back over what I'd just scrawled on the paper.

What came to mind as I reviewed the life lessons that I'd gleaned from the parable of Ladd's life, was a simple but unavoidable question:

If Ladd was such a dysfunctional man, addicted to alcohol, a neglectful father in a difficult marriage, obsessively buried in his work, and so easily embittered when he didn't get the scholarly respect he craved... could we actually learn anything of value from this guy?

I knew the answer, even before the question was fully formed in my mind: *Of course we can learn from Ladd's life, and his writings. After all, God uses broken people.* (What other kind does He have available?)

Noah, builder of the Ark (Gen. 6:8-8:22), later naked and drunk in the door of his tent (Genesis 9:20-23).

Abraham, father of a nation and receiver of the Covenant (Genesis 15), who had a regular habit of lying whenever he got into a tight spot (Genesis 20).

Moses, giver of the Law (Exodus 20-31), whose impudent disobedience kept him out of the Promised Land (Numbers 20:7-12).

Gideon, called by God to be Israel's deliverer (Judges 6:11-7:25), who later set up idols and led the recently-delivered Israelites to worship other gods instead of Yahweh (Judges 8:27).

Samson, uniquely gifted by God (Judges 13), yet so committed to his own selfish immaturity that he didn't even notice the Spirit had left him until it was too late, and he was blind and chained in a dungeon (Judges 16:20-21).

King David, Psalmist extraordinaire, the "man after God's own heart" (Acts 13:22), and his adultery with Bathsheba, with the shadow of her murdered husband hovering nearby (2 Samuel 11).

Elijah, considered the greatest of the Prophets, who was instrumental in a great spiritual victory on Mount Carmel (1 Kings 18:16-39): a few days later, he is depressed, whinging, and asking God to kill him (1 Kings 19:1-14).

James and John, part of Jesus' inner circle who were privileged to witness His Transfiguration (Mark 9:2-8), who mistook friendship with Jesus for an opportunity to grab positions of power and authority over their fellow disciples (Mark 10:35-40).

Peter, the Rock, the one with the revelation that Jesus was the promised Messiah (Matthew 16:13-20), and his thrice-established, swear-on-a-stack-of-Bibles denial that he even knew Jesus at all (Matthew 26:69-75).

The Bible is refreshingly candid about the failures and weaknesses of its heroes. The biography about George Eldon Ladd is of similar quality: Here is a theological giant whose influential writings have helped to shape our understanding of the Kingdom of God in a profound and inspiring way. And yet here also is a mere man, beset with human frailty, insecurities, and failures: as a husband, as a father, as a mentor, and in his long and losing battle with bitterness, depression, and alcoholism.

The breeze picked up suddenly, drawing my attention out of the journal with a much cooler caress. The sun was almost behind the mountains directly across from my vantage point. The seagulls were long gone. Clearly, it was time to wrap things up for the evening.

Pulling on my hoodie as I turned away from the darkening surface of the lake, I resolved to learn as much as I could from George Eldon Ladd. To learn from the sobering caution of his personal life, as well as digging deep into his books, especially his most influential: *The Presence of the Future*.

The sun was now completely behind the mountains, and the streetlights were already flickering into life, despite the relative earliness of the hour. That’s the way things are, when you live in the mountains. It's beautiful, but sunsets are quick and final, no matter what time of the year.

Quickening my pace towards the #11 bus stop, I wondered what the Younger and Elder had been up to since we parted ways. That thought alone brought a smile to my face, as I tucked the biography and my journal under my arm, and dug into my pocket for bus fare.

Further Conversations

1. The setting of this chapter is a lakeside park. It is the only outdoor setting in the book. Why would the author choose this setting to look deeper into Ladd's failures and weaknesses?
2. Where or to whom do you turn for comfort?
3. Whose opinion carries the most weight for you?
4. Have you ever been humiliated for standing up for what you thought was right?
5. In your experience, which element(s) in our current culture seem antithetical towards biblical Christianity as you see it?
6. After learning about Ladd's troubled life, how do you view his contribution to theological understanding?
7. Agree/Disagree: If Ladd had received a positive review from Norman Perrin, his life would have turned out completely different.

Extra Credit: *(the Elder made me call it that...)*

1. Find a copy of *A Place at the Table* and read the story of Ladd's life.
2. Do you know of other people who have had a troubled family/personal life and yet have made notable contributions to Christian thought and practice?

chapter Three
setting the table

The times, they are a-changing, the Elder thought to himself, as he strode through the impressive foyer of the high-rise apartment building and stepped into the elevator. Memories of days gone by, and of his own first apartment – the squeaky faucets, the faded cabinets in the kitchen, the cramped and creaking elevator – came nostalgically to mind as he marveled at the size, comfort, and gleaming interior of the elevator.

Rising almost silently through the lower floors, the elevator slid smoothly into position at his requested stop, the polished doors opening quietly and efficiently. Beyond, the warmly lit corridor beckoned the passengers to disembark to their destinations.

Stepping aside in a quaintly archaic and unconscious move of chivalry, the Elder allowed the other two passengers to exit ahead of him. Glancing once more around the gleaming interior, he collected his thoughts and stepped into the hallway. The carpet was a rich, dark green, with a cushion effect that he could feel even through his shoes. A mental image of the well-worn throw rug in his own living room flickered across his mind, and he smiled a nostalgic smile.

He found the address he was looking for just a short distance down the hall, to his left. Knocking sharply on the door, he waited for an answer from within, admiring once again the modern apartment building. The Elder was a genuinely contented man, and while he was impressed by his surroundings, it never occurred to him to make an unflattering comparison to his own modest dwelling in an older part of town.

"Good evening, professor!" announced the Younger, as he opened the door with a bow. "Welcome to my humble abode. I've already started cooking dinner, so come on in, and make yourself comfortable!"

The enticing aroma of frying onions and peppers greeted the Elder as he entered. With a flourish, the Younger took the Elder's coat and casually hung it – almost threw it, truth be told – onto the coat tree behind the door. The Elder, in true Canadian fashion, removed his shoes before following the Younger down the short hallway to the brightly-lit kitchen.

"You certainly have a modern building," commented the Elder, looking around the apartment with appreciation and interest. "Your elevator reminded me of the control panel in an airplane cockpit at first glance. I was afraid I might accidentally end up in orbit, or set off some alarms if I pushed the wrong button."

"That thought never occurred to me," replied the Younger, hiding a facetious expression as he resumed chopping vegetables. "I guess you're more used to the days of old when elevators had human operators. *'Which floor, sir?'*" he mimicked in a high, scratchy voice.

The Elder laughed, "You've been watching too many old cartoons, my young friend. I think you meant to say my *father* would have been more familiar with elevator operators." The wide array of cooking utensils around the Younger's kitchen was impressive, and the Elder appreciatively picked up one of the large cutting knives and tested its edge.

"Quite a collection you have here," he observed, replacing the knife carefully in the wooden knife block, next to its kin.

The Younger glanced up briefly as he added the vegetables to the sizzling contents of the wok on his stovetop. "When you enjoy cooking as much as I do, it's like having the right tools for the job. And I realized the other day that after all those years of you dropping by my Mom and Dad's house, I needed to invite you to see my new place." Wiping his hands on the towel draped over the oven door handle, he turned to face the Elder.

The Elder had continued to explore the utensils on the opposite counter and was now holding up a wicked-looking meat tenderizer. "Have you ever noticed how much one of these resembles an old-fashioned mace from medieval times?" he asked innocently. Without waiting for an answer, he began applying it with a respectable amount of force to a pair of steaks awaiting attention on the wooden cutting board. *Thwack.*

"Careful," warned the Younger, laughing nervously to cover his very real concern. "I don't know how well-made that counter is. I'm not sure the 'hammer of Thor' approach is what my cabinets need to experience. Or to survive, in this case."

"Hammer of Thor, eh?" mused the Elder, turning his attention with more carefully moderated force to the twin of the first steak. *Thwack.* "It *does* feel somewhat apocalyptic, now that you mention it."

They had been friends long enough that the Younger instantly recognized that the Elder had a metaphor cooking, in addition to their meal.

"Ah, so I see we're going to dive into a discussion about the Kingdom, right here in the kitchen," he observed, looking briefly over his shoulder to check on the sizzling contents of the wok. "So, now my meat tenderizer is 'apocalyptic'? A sign of the end of time?"

The Elder continued to work on the steaks with the tenderizing hammer. He was careful to not use excessive force, as per the Younger's request, yet the dull sound of the impact was accentuated by pauses in his speech.

"Why not... *(thwack)*? Table fellowship was where some of *(thwack)...* the most significant teachings of Jesus occurred – the 'Upper Room Discourse' *(thwack)...* in the Gospel of John, for example."

"And the apocalyptic understanding... *(thwack)* was one of the schools of thought in ancient Jewish culture... *(thwack)* around the time when Jesus began announcing 'the Kingdom is near'," he paused, looking over his shoulder. The Younger nodded in silent agreement, arms folded as he listened, and the Elder returned to his task. "And since our goal... *(thwack)* is to more fully understand what Jesus *meant* when He said 'the Kingdom is near'... *(thwack)* we should have a decent working understanding of what people in Jesus' day believed... *(thwack)* about the coming Kingdom."

"Yes, I remember reading something about that," agreed the Younger, turning to give the contents of his wok a quick stir. "The Israelites had the idea that Jesus was going to be a political messiah, but that wasn't what He really meant at all. They expected one thing, and Jesus gave them something completely different."

"Well, yes and no," the Elder conceded, finishing his assault on the steaks. "There were actually *several* different views of the Kingdom floating around at that time, all of which had an impact on the expectations of the people. We would do well to keep in mind, for example, that Israel was an occupied country in those days. Their hopes and expectations were that the Messiah would free them from the oppression of the Roman Empire."

"Sounds like you've been re-reading your Ladd," observed the Younger, gesturing with the wooden spoon he was using to stir the peppers, onions, and vegetables in the wok. "To be honest, I haven't read much of it, yet. Don't get me wrong: Ladd is obviously brilliant, but it's not exactly light bedtime reading. But I do recall him mentioning the differing expectations of the Israelites when Jesus first showed up."

The Elder set the meat tenderizer down on the counter, crossing the kitchen to open the refrigerator. Looking inside for the briefest of moments, he emerged with a bottle of *Salsa Picante*, which he placed on the counter next to the meat tenderizer. A clear-bodied saltshaker completed his tiny collection of elements.

"Let's use a few kitchen items as symbols for the differing schools of thought about the Kingdom in Jesus' time," he suggested, arranging his collection on the counter as the Younger watched with curiosity. "All of the ideas surrounding the Kingdom had a common understanding that the Kingdom of God occurred *within* history. The Israelites, because of their unique history, understood Jehovah as the *God who comes*. He is active in history, not detached from it."

"And Israel was also aware, because of God's promise to Abraham, that all nations would be blessed through them. And therefore, they also recognized that God's reign over His Kingdom would be contested by the other nations and whatever 'gods' they served," he concluded, singling out the bottle of *Salsa Picante*.

The Younger shrugged good-naturedly as he leaned closer. "The reign and rule of God as salsa? Why not? And let me guess: the tenderizer represents the apocalyptic, however you might define that?"

"Yes, but let's come back to that, shall we?" agreed the Elder, his hand still resting on the *Salsa Picante*. "Where this salsa becomes *picante* is in the concept of 'kingdoms in conflict', which is a historical understanding that Israel was very familiar with. From the Exodus out of Egypt on, the reign and rule of God was understood to be in conflict with the kingdoms created by human beings."

The Elder picked up the saltshaker next, gazing thoughtfully at it as he spoke. "The saltshaker, on the other hand, could represent the prophetic lens which the Israelites viewed history through." He shook the saltshaker gently as he continued, causing its contents to dance within. "Not prophecy in the sense of 'thus saith the Lord', but rather as the *ethical* dynamic which the Old Testament prophets held in such high and holy regard. And I use the word 'holy' quite deliberately."

The Elder's focus shifted to the face of his friend, although he continued to hold the saltshaker aloft between them. "If you read the prophetic books in the Old Testament, you could summarize their focus – without over-simplifying things – as the *ethical implications* of being the people of Yahweh. And conversely, how their failure as a nation to live by the Covenant they had with God (through Abraham) was the reason why Israel experienced exile and opposition."

The Younger opened the refrigerator once again, searching for and finding a bottle of barbeque sauce.

"Okay, so there's the kingdoms-in-conflict salsa, the saltshaker of ethics, and the meat tenderizer of the apocalypse," the Younger summarized. "Would you care to elaborate on the meat tenderizer? Oh, and by the way, thanks for *not* choosing this sauce as one of your object lessons. I have another use in mind for it, starting now."

Tucking the barbeque sauce under his arm, and gathering up the steaks, he opened a sliding door and stepped out onto the balcony. As he fired up his propane barbeque, he called back into the kitchen, "Could you bring two plates, please and thank you?"

The Elder followed him outside, plates in one hand, and the meat tenderizer in the other. "Well, when I say 'apocalypse', it's because that particular school of thought, and expectations, was very much focused on the *eschatological* implications of the Kingdom of God," he continued, barely missing a beat. "And by *eschatological* I mean, of course, that there is a *future* element to the Kingdom of God, beyond this world and time. Christians refer to it now as 'the second coming of Jesus', but the concept of an apocalyptic, earth-shattering event to usher in the Kingdom was also known in Jesus' day. The prophets called it 'the Day of the Lord', and it is a dominant theme in much of the Old Testament."

"And it's more optimistic than the Mayan version, which just had us all dead back in 2012," observed the Younger, as he adjusted the heat on the barbeque. The steaks began to make their own sizzling contribution to the conversation as the Younger seared the first side. "And let me guess: the expectation of an apocalypse of Kingdom Come probably contributed to the idea that Jesus was a political messiah, right? The Kingdom would break in with power, that'd be the end of the Roman occupation, and Israel would return to the glory days of old. How am I doing so far?"

"Exemplary," confirmed the Elder with a smile, although the Younger could tell by the tone of his admission that there was more yet to be said. "The *reason* why this apocalyptic, in-breaking power of the Kingdom was anticipated, or better yet, *yearned for*, was because they'd lost hope that society could be redeemed, even by God. They became so pessimistic about the state of society that they couldn't believe that it was even *worth* saving. Therefore, the coming of the Kingdom was expected be an apocalyptic, earth-shattering event, destroying the old order to make way for the new."

The Younger reached beneath the barbeque for his outdoor cooking utensils, flipping the steaks over and nodding with approval at the grill markings on each. "So, when you say they were 'pessimists', you don't mean they gave up on *God*. They just gave up on society in general."

"Exactly," agreed the Elder, leaning against the balcony railing. "As a result, they assumed that when the Kingdom came, it would result in Israel's enemies being destroyed, especially the current ones, the Romans. And with the Romans out of the way, Israel would regain its political, cultural, and religious freedom."

The Younger flipped the steaks a second time, lowering the heat, and applied a thin veneer of barbeque sauce with the brush strokes of an *artiste*. "And how does the saltshaker of ethics fit into all of this?"

"Well, that school of thought hadn't disappeared, but you have to remember, there had been *no prophets in Israel* for a long time," began the Elder, inhaling deeply as the mouth-watering aroma of the steaks filled the air. "When John the Baptist first appeared on the scene, the Israelites had just gone through what is known as the 'four hundred silent years', during which Yahweh hadn't spoken through a prophetic voice. That's why there was such a sense of anticipation when John began his ministry."

"But getting back to the Old Testament prophets, and their prophecies..."

The Elder briefly stepped into the kitchen, and returned with both the salsa and the saltshaker, which he placed on the little two-seater table on the balcony, next to the plates he'd brought out. "The prophets spoke on behalf of Yahweh, calling the people to honor their covenant with Him. They warned that if the covenant was broken – from Israel's end, not God's – then judgment would fall to get their attention, in order to turn them back to God. But if Israel would honor the covenant, then they would enjoy the blessings of God."

The Younger checked the steaks once more, noting their progress with satisfaction, and deftly flipped them again before applying more barbeque sauce. "So, let's see if I'm following your line of thought so far: the basic point of the prophets was: first, obey God and enjoy His Kingdom, and second, He is the God who *comes* to His people inside history, like He did with Moses when they were freed from Egypt. God would be part of their ongoing story, as long as they kept the covenant."

The Elder replaced the saltshaker on the little table, impressed. "You've got it. But the question that shaped the understanding of the apocalyptic school of thought was their belief that the Israelites, after their years in exile and leading up to John the Baptist and Jesus, *were* keeping the covenant. They were at a loss to explain why they were a conquered, occupied territory of the Roman Empire. As a nation, they were keeping their end of the bargain, so why wasn't the Kingdom coming?"

The Elder studied his collection of kitchen symbols for a moment before he continued. "Keep in mind, there was *always* an understanding that the 'Day of the Lord' would come in the future. It would be a time when God's Kingdom would be completely, thoroughly, universally established. All the schools of thought in Jesus' day agreed on this common understanding and expectation."

The Younger collected the steaks from the barbeque, placing them reverently on the plates. "So, their pessimism morphed into expecting a political Messiah because they figured they deserved the Kingdom?"

The Elder winced. "Well, we shouldn't be too harsh on them for thinking that way. They were simply attempting to make sense of the intersection between faith and history. Their example should provide a caution for us as well: how much of our theology is being influenced by our own culture? But that's a topic for another day," he concluded, smiling briefly before a quizzical look crossed his face. "What's that smell?"

The Younger frowned, perplexed for a moment as he sniffed the air, before a sudden horrifying realization came to him. "The wok! It's been on the stove all this time!"

The steaks were momentarily forgotten as the two dashed back into the kitchen, waving the smoke away as they entered. The Younger quickly removed the wok from the stovetop, turning off the heat, as the Elder hastened to open the windows.

"So much for the peppers, 'shrooms, and veggies," sighed the Younger, as the charred and unrecognizable mash smoked and cooled in the sink. "Maybe an un-tended wok would be a better symbol for the apocalypse," he suggested with an embarrassed grin. "It was sudden, dramatic, and definitely over-turned our expectations for the evening."

The Elder continued to fan the air with the tea towel, clearing the remnants of the smoke as best he could. "I'm impressed that you found a way to stay on topic. And it's interesting that you mentioned our expectations *not* being fulfilled as we anticipated," he observed thoughtfully. "I think it's worth pointing out that Jesus didn't *reject* the various schools of thought about the Kingdom that were floating around during His day. Instead, He *re-defined* – or re-directed – their expectations regarding the Kingdom."

The Younger disappeared for a moment, retrieving the steaks from the balcony. "I vote that we *not* neglect the part of our meal that we didn't torch by accident," he announced decisively, setting the aromatic plates on the table. "I think there's still a bowl of potato salad in the fridge. Will that do as a substitute? For eating, I mean, not as a Kingdom metaphor."

Guessing correctly which drawer held the cutlery, the Elder placed knives and forks on the table, as the Younger brought out the potato salad.

"I'm such a carnivore, I'd be happy just eating the steaks," admitted the Elder, as he nevertheless scooped a generous portion of potato salad onto his plate.

"But before we begin our meal, I'd like to toss out one last thought about the Kingdom, although we need to further unpack this conversation at a more opportune time."

"You mean we're *not* going to keep talking about the Kingdom while we're eating?" asked the Younger, genuinely surprised.

Maintaining a perfectly neutral expression, the Elder feigned innocence. "Doesn't your television work? And isn't there a hockey game on at this very moment? What better way to enjoy table fellowship?"

The Younger laughed as he retrieved the remote control from the glass-topped coffee table. "You, my friend, are a living example of a true fan. When people think 'hockey *fanatic*', your face should be what comes to mind. Okay, give me your last thought, before food and a hockey game steal our focus completely."

The Elder settled in at the table, carefully positioned with a clear view of the wide-screen television mounted on the wall. He was momentarily distracted as the image of his own 20-year-old television console set flashed through his mind, but recovered quickly and finished his thought.

"In my sometimes humble opinion, I think it would be wise to invest more time exploring the different schools of thought. It's such an important backdrop to Jesus' own teaching on the Kingdom, His own understanding of how and when the Kingdom comes, the ethics of the Kingdom, and so on," he began, taking up his knife and fork. "But to summarize: there is the saltshaker of the prophetic and ethical aspects, the salsa of the over-arching 'kingdoms in conflict', and the meat tenderizer, or the hammer of Thor, as you call it, of the apocalyptic, in-breaking, earth-changing Kingdom Come."

"Thank you, God, for good food and good friends to share it with," the Younger cheerfully prayed as he sat down beside his friend.

"Amen to that," agreed the Elder, as he began to cut industriously into his steak. "And let's keep in mind that Jesus repeatedly adjusted peoples' ideas and expectations to fit Kingdom *reality*, and as the King of the Kingdom, He would know."

"Gotcha," the Younger cheerfully responded, shifting his own chair to also face the television. "Jesus trumps expectation." Raising the remote control and pointing it at his home theatre, he slyly reminded the Elder of one last important facet to their discussion:

"By the way, if you'll wash, I'll dry."

"Done," agreed the Elder, already chewing with obvious contentment.

The Younger pressed the power button as they settled in for an extended time of table fellowship.

Further Conversations

1. What can you tell about the Younger's life and personality from his home? What does your home say about you?
2. Do you have objects in your home that are symbolic in that they remind you of something else?
3. Now that the three symbols have been introduced, stop right now and get one of each (or nearest equivalent). From now on, have them on the table when discussing this book. *(Yeah, seriously.)*
   (a) Which symbol do you think would be the most offensive to our current culture?
   (b) Which symbol do you think would be the most exciting to the church?
   (c) Which symbol (and the topic it symbolizes) are you the most curious about?
4. Agree/Disagree: The kingdom of God is mainly about (a) angels and demons, (b) the end of the world, or (c) living ethically. (And tell us why.)

<u>Extra Credit:</u>

1. Find a list of Old Testament prophecies about the coming of the Messiah. Also, make a list of all the times that Jesus used the phrase: "Kingdom of God". Keep these lists on hand for the upcoming chapters.

chapter Four
saltshaker

The late afternoon sun slanted in through the windows near the ceiling on the west wall, casting a warm glow across the highly polished wood above the bar, and glinting sharply on the various bottles on display. The Barkeep, as faithfully methodical as the antique clock ticking behind him, glanced briefly up at the shaft of warm light as he nursed a pint of Ireland's finest into a waiting glass.

"Guinness up!" he announced brusquely, his accent clearly betraying his Dublin origins. His love for his ancestral land could be clearly heard in his oft-spoken opinion that "ye haven't truly had Guinness, 'less ye can see the smokestacks o' Dublin."

"I've got it," called the familiar voice of his wife, as she saw the other waitress already engaged in lively banter with a large group of businesspeople who had pulled two tables together to accommodate the size of their party. The Barkeep watched her with fondness as she scooped up the tray of pints and carried them with practiced ease through the crowded pub.

It wasn't the first time he'd been reminded of just how much he appreciated his wife's presence in the bar. He might be the Barkeep, but she was the Proprietress, the real power behind the business end of things. They had settled into a comfortable partnership over the years: he was content to be the public face behind the bar, while his wife employed her considerable business savvy to ensure their joint venture remained profitable.

The Proprietress returned and placed the now-emptied tray on the bar counter, just as the door opened behind her, allowing two familiar figures to enter. Rejoicing over their good fortune at finding their favorite booth available (the one in the corner, with the window overlooking the street and the well-treed park), they eagerly laid claim to it.

It seemed to the Barkeep that the two of them were always energized about something. He tried in vain to recall an instance when they weren't, and quickly gave up.

"Keep yer eye on those two," he commented gruffly to the Proprietress, nodding in their direction, as the Younger and the Elder hung their jackets on the coat-hooks adorning the outside rim of their booth. "Once they get into it, they get loud."

"Do they now?" countered the Proprietress, leaning her arm on the top of the bar as she stole a measuring look at the two rabble-rousing newcomers. Turning back to her burly husband, she asked, "Do they drink too much, or do they just like to fight? Or maybe a wee bit o' both?"

The Barkeep shook his head, resuming his unconscious habit of wiping down his work area. "No, no, nothing like that. They're just... well, *religious* folk, and don't ask me why, but they love coming in here to have their talks."

"Well, better that, than the likes o' them," she replied sharply, gesturing with a nod of her head towards the table of inebriated businesspeople, who had finally released the afternoon waitress from their conversation. "They're regulars, too, but I've been *this close*," she gestured with her thumb and forefinger barely an inch apart, "to throwing the lot o' them out, more than once."

"Well, the night is young," quipped the Barkeep, as the hint of a smile teased at one side of his mouth. He began pouring another Guinness. "Those nice church gents will be wanting one o' these, and the younger one will want an ale he can see through. And more'n' likely, they'll be asking for curry fries about five minutes after they get their beer."

He glanced up at the Proprietress with a wink. "They're rather... *religious* about it."

"Oh, aren't we clever tonight?" teased his wife, as she swatted him on the arm with the cloth he had been wiping the counter with. And as the stout ale swirled in the glass, they shared a comfortable laugh together, one born more of many years of comradeship, rather than the cleverness of the Barkeep's joke.

The sound of their laughter carried over to the occupants of the corner booth.

"What do you suppose they find so funny?" wondered the Younger, shifting about on the wooden bench, instinctively searching out the most comfortable position. "You haven't worn that old fedora of yours in months."

"Ah, the egocentrism of youth," countered the Elder, as he adjusted the placement of his utensils, ignoring the subtle dig at his favorite hat. "Why must we assume that their laughter has anything at all to do with us? I, for one, am quite content to think that they are simply enjoying their work. And that they get to do it together."

"I, for one, am grateful that she isn't anywhere near as crusty as our Irish Barkeep," laughed the Younger. "I'd think it would take a special woman to be married to someone like him."

"Spoken like an unmarried man," replied the Elder, in equal parts jesting and seriousness. "If there's anything I learned from my beloved wife, it is that *all* women are 'special', to put up with the likes of our gender. When you finally find that certain someone, you'll know what I mean. More than anyone else on this planet, my wife was the instrument of God in my life, rounding off my rough edges, and encouraging me to be the man God wanted me to be."

The Younger was unsure how to respond, sadly mindful of the Elder's sudden and tragic loss, not quite three years previous. "I also believe," continued the Elder, "to be honest if not completely modest, that God used me in her life, as well. 'Iron sharpens iron', as they say. Even in marriage; maybe *especially* in marriage," he concluded with a smile.

The two of them suddenly noticed the Proprietress standing near their booth, balancing a tray crowded with drinks with the ease that comes from years of experience. How long she had been waiting, clearly having overheard their conversation, neither of them knew for certain, Seeing their gaze turn to her, she quickly set the tray down on their table, placing the Guinness before the Elder and the Alexander Keith's IPA in front of the Younger.

"Home is where they know ye," she offered in response to their unspoken question, gesturing over her shoulder in the general direction of her husband. "At least, that's what *he* says." And with that, she turned abruptly and continued to serve the remaining drinks on her tray to other waiting customers at their respective booths and tables.

"I guess when they know which pints to deliver, it's a sign that we've officially become regulars at this pub," suggested the Younger, as he took an appreciative swig of his ale. "And, perhaps, that we're also creatures of habit."

The Elder admired the opaque darkness of his stout before also taking a sip. "There are good habits as well as bad," he observed, as he reached into his weathered leather satchel. Mindful of the location of his almost-full pint on the table, he placed his well-worn copy of *Jesus and the Kingdom* in front of him, its pages bristling with makeshift bookmarks from his recent readings. "And since lively theological discourse is one of our better habits, what say we invest our time accordingly?"

The Younger quickly burrowed into his messenger bag ("It's not a purse," he would stubbornly insist, "it's a *messenger bag.*"), and brought out a thin, leather-bound electronic device. Tapping the screen into wakefulness, he called up the file he was looking for.

The Elder stared in wonderment, speechless for a moment. "Are you quite serious?" he finally managed. "You have Ladd's books stored on that tiny little contraption of yours?"

The Younger looked mildly offended. "What did you think I had on this? Marvel comic books? I've got commentaries, a bunch of different Bible translations, *and* a whole pile of Christian classics; perhaps you've heard of Anselm, Jerome or Bernard of Clairvaux? And, last but certainly not least, a certain book by George Eldon Ladd: *The Presence of the Future*."

The Elder looked suitably impressed, turning a few of the dog-eared pages of his own copy, the creases and thumb-stained edges suddenly more pronounced than he'd remembered. Looking up as another thought occurred to him, he started to ask a question, but was cut off instantly by the Younger.

"No," he admitted candidly, "I haven't read them all yet. But now that you've got me into reading classic theology, I may be developing a new addiction. It takes awhile to adjust to the way that they use the English language, but it's like reading *A Tale of Two Cities* -- once you get into the author's rhythm, you can't stop."

"Can you also underline quotes, or should I say *highlight*, in that thing?" the Elder asked, gesturing toward the device. As the Younger quickly demonstrated several digital pages that included yellow highlights that he'd inserted, the Elder held up both of his hands with a chuckle. "I give up. You young people never cease to amaze me. And who says we don't have scribes anymore? It must have taken someone a great deal of time to transpose those classics into digital form."

"I hadn't thought about that part," replied the Younger, pausing for another sip of his ale. "But I'm glad that they did. Unless somebody re-publishes these old books, it's hard to track down decent copies that don't cost an arm and a leg."

"And just for the record," he added, again with a sheepish grin, "I can 'write in the margins' of my own books with this. So, now your books are safe."

The Elder was still so impressed by the versatility of the Younger's electronics that he didn't even flinch at the reminder of the unfortunate events that transpired the last time he'd loaned the Younger a cherished part of his personal library.

"Well, now that you've thoroughly fossilized me," sighed the Elder, "why don't we start unpacking the ideas of the Kingdom which we began to talk about at your apartment last week?" Reaching to his left, the Elder plucked the saltshaker out of the modest array of condiments on their table, and positioned it front and center between himself and the Younger.

“I’d like to suggest looking at the saltshaker first,” he began, as he flipped through the pages of his book, pausing to drink from his pint. “As I understand Ladd, the prophetic school of thought was the dominant one for many years, even after the addition of the apocalyptic school of thought. I’ve always found it reassuring to realize that the Old Testament prophets were not simply judgmental and negative; they were calling their fellow Israelites to live ethically as was proper for people of the Covenant.”

The Younger moved his pint a safe distance to the left of his e-reader. “Yeah, I was really intrigued by Ladd’s focus on the prophecies in the Old Testament. I mean, the prophets did speak ‘thus saith the Lord’ kinds of prophecies, but the content of their prophecies really had more to do with the ethics of God’s people. It’s sort of a ‘how then shall we live’ moment, Old Testament style.”

The Elder nodded, indicating the little saltshaker between them. “The prophetic school of thought believed that once Israel was properly obedient to the Covenant, then they could legitimately expect that they would inherit the Kingdom when the Messiah came. That’s why they emphasized obedience to the Law so strongly; it was their only hope to inherit.”

The Elder paused for a moment to sip his Guinness, recalling the yellow markings he’d seen in the Younger’s digital copy just moments earlier. “I’m curious to hear some of your observations," he said, mindful of the fresh and insightful comments the Younger was known for. "What stood out to you, when you first read Ladd?"

In response, the Younger drew his finger across the screen repeatedly, and the Elder marveled at the technology. "Well, you know how pragmatic I am," began the Younger, "always looking for the 'so what' question. Or the application, I guess I should say. And it was helpful, as you said, to learn that the prophets weren't all gloom and doom, just for the sake of being gloom and doom. But I did find something in Ladd that I wasn't expecting."

Finding the page he was looking for, he held up the e-reader and quoted,

> "The Biblical idea of redemption always includes the earth. Hebrew thought saw an essential unity between man and nature. The prophets do not think of the earth as merely the indifferent theater on which man carries out his normal task but as the expression of the divine glory."[1]

The Younger replaced the e-reader on the table, and met the gaze of the Elder. "I guess I was a little surprised, to be honest, to find the idea of 'creation care' in a book written almost half a century ago. Maybe it's part of that 'egocentrism of youth' that you mentioned earlier, and I hate to admit it, but I would have thought it was mostly my generation that was concerned about our responsibility to take care of the environment – God's creation."

"Every generation thinks it's special," soothed the Elder, recalling his own youth with amusement. "You would be amazed, and I would be embarrassed, if you could have heard some of the fiery rhetoric from when my friends and I considered ourselves the rabid revolutionaries of our day." He chuckled ruefully at the memory.

"So, you mentioned having a 'so what' question. Could you be more specific?"

"Well, like I said, I'm always looking for the practical application," repeated the Younger, absent-mindedly adjusting the placement of various items on his side of the table. "And caring for the environment is something that I wish more Christians would take seriously."

The Elder nodded in understanding. "It helps to remember that Ladd was writing partly to refute the 'it's all going to burn anyway' mentality that was prevalent in his day. So, it's not surprising that he reminded us about the groundwork for Christian responsibility to exercise what we used to call 'stewardship' of the earth."

"What you may find helpful," the Elder continued, after another sip of his pint, "is to do a bit of research in the Old Testament on the importance of 'the land', including the seven year agrarian cycle that is actually part of their written Law.

"It's really a blueprint for, to borrow your phrase, 'creation care'. And there are a number of warnings of impending judgment *against* the people of Israel for not being proper stewards of the land."

The Younger placed his e-reader on the table, carefully avoiding the beads of condensation left by his pint of ale. "Actually, I *do* remember the emphasis placed on 'the land'. But for some reason, I hadn't made the connection to today's environmental issues. Maybe because it was right next to rules and regulations on how to slaughter goats," he concluded with a grin.

The Elder smiled in return, and picked up the saltshaker again, leaning forward. "And it also ties nicely into the theme of Yahweh being the 'God who comes'. The common understanding that existed when Jesus first appeared was that God is not detached from history. Throughout the entire history of the Israelite nation, from Abraham to the Exodus, from the time of Elijah and through all the prophetic promises of the Kingdom, we find this understanding that God comes within history. God is not an absentee parent; He is involved with His creation."

The Elder paused to quickly page through his book again, looking for the right bookmark. "Ah, here we go. This is important, too, I think:

> **"The prophetic expectation cannot be described as "historical" or "this-worldly" in the sense that it looks for the Kingdom of God to be the product of historical forces. The source of God's Kingdom is supra-historical; God himself must visit his people."[2]**

The Elder lowered the book to the table, and raised his eyes to meet the Younger's. "It's important because we need to keep these two ideas in tension: we are called to steward the earth because it was part of our mandate ever since the Garden of Eden, however, *we don't bring the Kingdom.* We are stewards, or perhaps 'caretakers' is a better word, of whatever God gives us. But it is God who comes to us, and He brings the Kingdom."

The Younger leaned back against the wooden bench, letting out a long, slow breath – a soundless whistle. "You're right, that *is* an important distinction. If I can be my usual pragmatic self, I'd say understanding that tension would," and he began to enumerate each point on his fingers, "first of all, give us a greater sense of a Creation Mandate: to 'steward' the earth, to use your phrase, and secondly, give us a good dose of humility about our own importance. Even in the midst of all our efforts to be good and faithful caretakers, we aren't capable of bringing the Kingdom. Only God can."

The Elder nodded, pleased at the insights his young friend was so quickly discovering. *It's amazing how investing in a bit of background reading could have such an impact on our discussion,* he thought to himself. He hadn't read Ladd in years, and he was grateful for the opportunity to revisit his theological roots.

Gesturing with the saltshaker, still held aloft in his left hand, the Elder steered the conversation back to its symbolic meaning. "Let's not lose sight of our original goal: to understand the Kingdom expectations of society when Jesus first appeared."

The Younger abruptly changed his position from reclining against the bench, to now leaning forward, arms folded on the table. “Okay, back to that. Let me see if I can summarize: the concern of the Old Testament prophets was on the ethical conduct of the Israelites. Basically, if they would honor the covenant with Yahweh, they would receive the Kingdom when it came. But if they *didn't* keep the covenant, the Kingdom will still come, but there would be no benefit to them.”

The Elder nodded, again impressed. “That's essentially it. The concept of a ‘righteous remnant’, or an ‘Israel within Israel’, is consistent throughout the Old Testament. You can see it when God reminds a very depressed Elijah that he wasn't the only one left. God said he reserved seven thousand who had not bowed to Baal: a ‘remnant’ within Israel, spiritually considered as the ‘real’ Israel. Their allegiance was critical – were they serving Yahweh or Baal? And the proof of where their loyalties truly lay was their obedience to the Law, the blueprint for their ethics.”

The Younger stirred in his chair as a possible objection occurred to him. “Yes, I'm familiar with some examples of people being asked to choose their allegiance. For example, Moses saying ‘who is on the Lord's side’[3], or Joshua saying ‘as for me and my house, we will serve the Lord’[4]. And to use your example, Elijah saying ‘if the Lord is God, serve Him’[5]. But...”

He leaned even further forward, his eyebrows knit together in concentration. “There were also prophecies about people doing all the right things, but their hearts not being in it. And that meant the outward ‘proof’ of their allegiance to God was useless, a fraud. ‘Away with the noise of your worship', I think the phrase was. I forget which prophet said that."

The Elder smiled, spreading his hands wide. "And so we come to living in the tension between two truths: our ethical behavior is absolutely important, but our heart attitude must also be right. And it was the prophet Amos you were quoting[6], I believe, although he wasn't the only one to sound that alarm. Isaiah also had some choice words about people honoring God with their lips, but their hearts being far from Him[7]. And Isaiah also records some strong words from God about how 'true worship' has a justice element to it, which I think your generation places a wonderful emphasis on.[8]"

The Younger eased back in the bench with a laugh, shaking his head. "Well, I'm feeling challenged and inspired. Seriously, I'm not joking," he hastened to add in response to the quizzical expression on the Elder's face. For a second time, he began to count off items on his fingers: "So far, we've talked about being stewards of creation, the righteous remnant within the nation of Israel, the importance of heart-felt loyalty and obedience, and that it is God who ultimately brings the Kingdom within human history. Is there anything else this modest little symbol has to tell us?" He ended with another laugh, gently tapping the saltshaker with his forefinger.

The Elder chuckled as he returned the saltshaker to its normal station in life, nestled between the pepper mill and the bottle of malt vinegar, all cuddled up next to the napkin dispenser. "Well, it's important to keep in mind that, as

Ladd so aptly puts it:", and he glanced down at his book as he read,

> "The fundamental ground of the Old Testament hope is its faith in God who reveals himself dynamically in history."[9]

He looked up from the pages as he continued. "The people who were alive in Jesus' time were all expecting that someday, somehow," and the Elder paused between each of the next three words for added emphasis, "God. Was. Coming."

"They may have lost a sense of 'it could happen any second', after four hundred years with no prophetic voices," the Elder continued, "but deep down, there was the expectation that the God who had come into their history before, was going to come again.

"And the prophetic school of thought emphasized the observance of the Law of Moses as the key to inheriting the Kingdom when the Messiah would come. It would be difficult to overstate how profound this hope was, especially under Roman occupation. And speaking of the Roman occupation, that is the perfect segue into talking about the apocalyptics and *their* expectations about the coming Kingdom."

Smiling, the Elder reached down into his satchel, and withdrew an item folded in oilcloth. Unwrapping the object with exaggerated ceremony, the Elder at last produced a wicked-looking, very large meat cleaver.

Out of the corner of his eye, the Younger saw the Proprietress jolt upright, an expression of incredulous concern on her face. The Younger could only stare in shock, dumbstruck, as the Elder good-humoredly brandished the cleaver in front of him.

"Are you kidding me?" the Younger gasped, finding his voice again. "You seriously brought a *meat cleaver* into a pub? And would you quit *waving it around?*" He schooled himself to not look in the direction of the Proprietress, who was now vigorously tugging on the Barkeep's shirtsleeve.

"Why not?" countered the Elder, oblivious to the drama developing behind the bar. "I liked your 'Hammer of Thor' meat tenderizer as a metaphor for the apocalyptics, but I don't own one. But then I spotted this old cleaver in my kitchen, and I immediately thought it would serve as a worthy substitute."

Shaking his head in disbelief, the Younger grabbed a menu with some haste from behind the condiments and napkin dispenser. "Well, you'd better order something, quick," he stage-whispered, as his eyes hurriedly scanned the menu, "because that waitress is on her way back, and she looks like a woman on a mission."

"Excellent," smiled the Elder, casually setting the cleaver on the table and reaching for his own menu. "I'm feeling rather hungry, myself."

Saltshaker Notes

1. George Eldon Ladd, *The Presence of the Future: the Eschatology of Biblical Realism*, (William B. Eerdmans Publishing Company, Grand Rapids Mich., 1974), 59
2. *Ibid.*, 58
3. Story told in Exodus 32; specific quote is verse 26
4. Story told in Joshua 24:1-27; specific quote is verse 15
5. Story told in 1 Kings 18:16-46; specific quote is verse 21
6. Prophecy told in Amos 5:21-24; specific quote is verse 23
7. Prophecy told in Isaiah 29; specific quote is verse 13
8. Isaiah 58 (the whole chapter – read it!)
9. *The Presence of the Future*, 52

Further Conversations

1. Now our friends are at their 'traditional' pub, and you have met the Barkeep and the Proprietress. What one word would you use to describe the bartender's attitude towards their two customers? What word would his wife choose?

2. Remember the meat cleaver? Have you ever done something that could be summed up as "When Dumb Things Happen to Smart People"? Tell us your story.

3. If you were in an Irish/Scottish/English style pub, what would you order? Would you play it safe or would you try something new?

4. Ethical implications: Where do I shop? How do I eat? What about inhumane growing and slaughter conditions? What about pesticide/herbicide use or GMO products? Are these questions that a Christian should be concerned with?

5. If the church is unified and holy will the kingdom come? What is God waiting for?

6. Our beliefs, sexuality and nationality have traditionally been central to our identities. Increasingly, how we eat and how we make purchasing decisions have become identity markers. How would you identify yourself if limited to 6 words? Include ethical choices.

7. Agree/Disagree: It is possible to disagree with someone's lifestyle without judging them.

Extra Credit:

1. Read Isaiah 58 (the whole thing - powerful stuff!)
2. What are the properties of Salt? How was it used in ancient times? When Jesus refers to salt in His stories, what does He mean?

chapter Five

thor's hammer

"Good Lord," gasped the Proprietress, reaching blindly behind her in an attempt to gain her husband's attention. "What's that he's got in his hand? Is that a meat cleaver? What kind of religion did you say they were?"

Her flailing grasp found the sleeve of the Barkeep's shirt, and she tugged on it with a great deal of insistence, her eyes riveted all the while on the two troublemakers in the corner booth.

The Barkeep leaned on the bar with both fists curled and at the ready, although he would later admit that he was somewhat mystified at the intensity of his wife's reaction. The two in the corner booth were sometimes a wee bit loud, but they'd never been any real trouble before. More like a mild nuisance, easily dealt with by a few choice words from him, when necessary.

Peering closely at the metal object the older gentleman had placed on the table, the Barkeep remained calm, although he didn't take his eyes off the booth. "Aye, it's a cleaver," he growled, keeping his voice down, mindful of the full crowd in the pub. "Beats me why he's brought it here, but they're harmless, those two."

The expression on his wife's face eloquently called into question his definition of "harmless", but she relaxed slightly and released her grip on his shirtsleeve. "Well, what should we do? Ring the police, just in case?"

Now it was his turn to give her an incredulous look. "Don't be daft! We don't need the police barging in here, givin' this place a bad name! Go see if they want something to eat," he concluded, gesturing towards the corner booth. "And don't draw attention to nothing."

My, how chivalrous of you, the Proprietress almost said aloud, as she gathered her wits about her. She briefly considered bringing something hard and metal with her, but thought better of it.

The Barkeep kept his eye on the corner booth, ready to intervene at a moment's notice, but he couldn't bring himself to believe anything more serious than a misunderstanding could be happening. *Those two can be a wee bit odd every now and then*, he reasoned to himself, *but they've never been, well, dangerous.*

After a few minutes of animated conversation, the Proprietress returned to the bar, her facial expression and body language communicating relief and a significantly lower blood pressure level. And, the Barkeep noted, the two occupants in the corner booth appeared properly penitent.

"What was the fuss all about?" he asked, still keeping his eyes on the booth.

His wife tried to think of a brief summary, but finally threw up her hands in exasperation. "I don't get religious people," she fumed. "All this talk about symbols and such. Anyway, they've ordered food, after all. At least that's something I *can* deal with."

Relieved but not overly surprised, the Barkeep chuckled as he returned to polishing his counter. "Don't tell me, let me guess. Two plates of curry fries, eh?"

"Not even close," his wife shot back, still steaming. "Fish and chips for the pale ale kid, and neeps 'n' tatties for the old beggar, or uncle, or whatever he is." And she disappeared abruptly through the kitchen door to inform the cook. The door swung vigorously after her spirited push.

The Barkeep smiled to himself, as the kitchen door swung shut behind her. *She's every bit as feisty as folk liked to say the Irish are*, he mused. And from the sound of things, she would be fired up about the two in the booth for a while yet, he'd wager.

Across the room, the Younger collected the menus together and replaced them behind the napkin dispenser with a sigh. For his part, the Elder wore the chagrined expression of a scolded schoolboy who'd just been given a vigorous tongue-lashing from the school principal.

"I can't believe you brought something so medieval-looking into a pub, without thinking how it might look to other people," exclaimed the Younger, gesturing to the cleaver. “Especially the Barkeep. *And* his sharp-tongued business partner.”

The Elder still seemed somewhat deflated by their recent encounter with the Proprietress. “She certainly has a way with words, doesn’t she?” he observed with sheepish admiration. “And I would describe her as a clear and effective communicator, indeed.”

He started to chuckle, but immediately stifled his mirth as he stole a glance towards the kitchen door, wary of the watchful eyes of the Proprietress.

“I can tell she’d rattled you,” observed the Younger with a bemused smile, “because you love meat, but you forgot to order any. I’ll think of you while I'm enjoying my fish and chips.”

“Look on the bright side,” countered the Elder, as he began to recover his usual good humor, “because neeps and tatties are traditionally served with *haggis*, my young culinary genius.”

The Younger screwed up his face in disgust. “You can call them ‘neeps and tatties’ all you want, but it’s just a clever attempt at disguising turnip and potatoes. You know, there’s a *very good reason* why they usually serve haggis with a shot of whiskey. It’s either to get your courage up before eating the haggis, or – more likely, in my opinion – to kill the aftertaste.”

The Elder shook his head with a long-suffering sigh, further evidence of his recovery after the pointed conversation with the Proprietress. “Good Scottish whiskey is a reward unto itself," he corrected, peering sternly over the top of his reading glasses. "And not merely as post-haggis mouthwash."

The Younger's gaze wandered to the meat cleaver – still on the table, but now at least partially camouflaged with a napkin, as per the inflexible demand of the Proprietress. "People usually call you a trouble-maker for something you've said, not for bringing kitchen weapons into a pub," he sighed in amazement. "If you'd phoned me, I could have brought my tenderizer. It's still a little medieval-looking, but not as threatening as your cleaver."

The Elder glanced briefly at the offending utensil, nestled close by the condiments and the napkin dispenser, as far from public view as possible. "At least she didn't confiscate it," he agreed. "Although I must confess, I'm somewhat disappointed that she didn't appreciate our symbolic use of it in our discussion about the Kingdom. But then again, we *are* treading water in a fairly deep theological sea."

"And on that note," smiled the Younger, referring once more to his electronic copy, "weren't you just about to dive into the Meat Cleaver of the Apocalypse understanding of the Kingdom?"

The Elder sat up a little straighter, thankful for the return to their previous discussion. "I feel a bit like Jesus, speaking with the rich young ruler, when He asked 'what is in the law? How do you read it?' It sounds like you've already got something in mind. Did something catch your attention as you were reading?"

"Guilty as charged," grinned the Younger. "I remembered your comment in my apartment about the apocalyptics *not* losing their faith that God would come, but just becoming pessimistic about the state of the world. And then I read this:

> "While nature and history were under the divine sovereignty, both lay under the curse of sin and the burden of evil. God's Kingdom would be established only by an in-breaking of God into history which would result in both a moral and a physical transformation of the present order."[1]

The Younger looked up, gazing at the trees in the park, directly across the street from their window-side booth. "The apocalyptics were on the same page as the prophetic, saltshaker school of thought in some ways: God is the God who comes to His people, and would establish His Kingdom when He came. But where they differed was on *how* the Kingdom would finally come."

Looking back at his friend once more, the Younger frowned thoughtfully as he chose his next words with care. "The prophetic side focused on being the kind of righteous people who would inherit the Kingdom when it came. But the apocalyptics viewed the world as so corrupted that it was more like God was *rescuing* them from the world, when the Kingdom came."

The Elder nodded in agreement, adding his own thoughts to the Younger's idea. "They were attempting to understand how Israel could return from exile, finally live in obedience to the Law of the Covenant, and yet not see the Kingdom come. And to make matters worse, no new prophets had spoken in about four hundred years, *and* they were now an occupied country under the brutal heel of the Roman Empire. Their development of a more apocalyptic, *catastrophic* view of the in-breaking of the Kingdom made the most sense to them, and shouldn't be surprising to us."

The Younger shifted again in his seat, placing one arm over the back of the bench. "So, in their view, the world had become so evil that the only way it could be redeemed was for God's intervention and complete transformation of..." he gestured helplessly, "well, *everything*."

"The Day of the Lord," agreed the Elder. "They saw the establishment of the Kingdom as the only hope for Israel. Their view of what it meant for Yahweh to be 'the God who comes' started to shift to something new. Here's another quote for you, which confirms what you just said:

> **"God is the God who will come; he is no longer God who comes to his people in history. The apocalyptists do not view the coming of the Kingdom as the final act of God who is constantly acting in history."[2]**

The Elder glanced up, eager to make his point. "You see? The difference was on *how* the Kingdom would come, as you said, but even deeper than that, *why* the Kingdom will come with such force, and bring total transformation. Instead of God coming *within* their history, as part of their story, He would instead *invade* history from the outside. So, when Jesus announced the Kingdom was near, they became excited because it was going to be a 'big bang' effect, especially on their hated oppressors, the Roman Empire."

Pausing briefly, the Elder quietly added for emphasis, "And once again, we mustn't be too harsh on the first century Israelites for their expectations. They based their beliefs on the Old Testament prophets, and now they were trying to make sense of the gap between the prophecies and their actual experience. Jesus *did* re-define or re-direct a number of their assumptions, to be sure, but if we are at all humble, we will recognize that we are equally capable of making the same mistakes."

And with that reminder, the Elder continued reading:

> "The solution to the problem of evil was thrown altogether into the future. The present is irremediably evil, and the righteous can only submit patiently to suffering, sustained by the assurance that deliverance will surely come when the evil age is over and the new age of the Kingdom arrives."[3]

The Younger whistled in amazement. "That really *does* sound like some Christians I know. I guess the 'it's all gonna burn, anyway' mentality isn't new, after all."

The Elder was clearly picking up steam, eager to explore further. "And just like the modern-day apocalyptics, who have decided there's nothing to do but endure until God breaks in, *they made the Kingdom all about them*. For the first century Israelites, it was all about their nation, their piety, and their rescue from evil and from their Roman oppressors. And we all-too-often have the same mentality today. Yet Jesus made it abundantly clear that it was *His* Kingdom, coming on *His* terms, and that it would come in a way which would confound their expectations completely."

He paused in mid-thought, as they both became acutely aware of the return of the Proprietress. The tray she was carrying, perfectly balanced and rock-steady in her grip, was heavily laden with multiple food orders. They both fell immediately and uncharacteristically silent, their only action consisting in cautiously moving their books out of her way.

"Fish 'n' chips, and a plate o' neeps 'n' tatties," she announced, deftly placing each of the meals before the appropriate diner. "Will either of you gents be wanting anything else?"

"No, this will do just fine," managed the Elder, not looking directly at her, still somewhat embarrassed about his earlier *faux pas* with the meat cleaver. Furtively, his left hand tugged the napkin further over its conspicuous wood-and-metal handle.

"I'm good," agreed the Younger meekly, doing his best to look self-confident and yet inoffensive at the same time. They both murmured their thanks to her, as she favored them with a final look that was clearly meant as a reminder of who the boss was, before she abruptly turned away and moved on to the next table.

Once satisfied that she was out of hearing range, the Elder spoke again. “While I regret being the cause of such an uproar, I really *do* like the symbolism of using a meat cleaver for the apocalyptics.” And as he spoke, he gently patted the offending symbol under its cloth camouflage.

“Because the expectation of the apocalyptics,” he continued, “was that the coming of the Kingdom would be a dramatic, earth-shattering, cataclysmic event. Their political ideal was that Israel would become the head and not the tail, so to speak, a complete reversal on the Roman Empire. To them, the ‘Day of the Lord’ was going to be every bit as fiery and bombastic as anything they’d read in Isaiah or Ezekiel. The ‘hammer of Thor’, as you so eloquently described my cooking technique.”

The Younger nodded, chewing with great enthusiasm. “I noticed something similar in Ladd’s comments on the book of IV Ezra,” he added, speaking carefully around a particularly juicy morsel. “Even though it’s not part of the Bible, it still reflected their understanding at the time.” Glancing to his right, he read:

> **“The only hope lies in the future. By divine decree, there are two ages: the present age is hopelessly evil, but the future age will witness the solution to the problem of evil.”[4]**

“Ah, yes,” agreed the Elder, dining with equal enthusiasm on his unintentionally vegetarian meal (a rare occasion, as he would freely admit.) “You’ll notice the same theme throughout the New Testament as well: ‘this present age' and 'the age to come'. It's as common a concept in both Testaments as was the concept of the 'righteous remnant'."

The Younger finished his meal with a flourish, dabbing at the corners of his mouth with his napkin. "I didn't realize how hungry I really was, until my meal showed up," he admitted, sighing contently. Tucking his napkin under the edge of his plate, he picked up his e-reader once more. "I know we still have to discuss your jar of *salsa picante*," he hesitated briefly, as if half expecting the Elder to pull a jar from his sleeve, "but I can't move on until we've looked at some practical applications."

The Elder paused, fork halfway to his mouth as he replied, "For the record, I thought we could substitute a bottle of ketchup for the *salsa picante*. It was only the wonderful symbolism of the meat tenderizer that inspired me to bring my cleaver in its place." Remembering his fork in mid-air, he took another bite of his food. "And I'm always in favor of being practical, instead of merely theoretical. So, what applications do you see here?"

The Younger switched over to the notes he'd written down earlier, during his research. "Well, just like the saltshaker school of thought, we should have a much humbler view of our own importance in the grand scheme of things. I mean, it's not about asking God to bless *our* mission, it's about us getting on board with *His* mission."

The Elder finished his meal, arranging his knife and fork at the 'four o'clock' position, and sliding his plate towards to outside edge of the booth. The Younger watched with bemused interest.

"Why do you do that?" he asked, not unkindly. "Do you think it really makes any difference how you oh-so-meticulously arrange your cutlery on the plate once you're finished eating?"

As if on cue, the Proprietress materialized at their booth, deftly scooping up the Elder's plate, cutlery and all. "Can I get anything else for you?" she asked, her tone of voice noticeably more moderated compared to their earlier conversation about the cleaver.

"Dessert? More ale? Are you finished, or not?" That last question was directed solely at the Younger, as she indicated his plate with a nod of her head.

"Uh, yeah, I'm finished," agreed the subdued Younger, quickly re-arranging his cutlery. "And coffee would be great, thank you."

"One for me, as well," added the Elder. "Black, the way God drinks it."

The Younger hastened to request cream and sugar, and as the Proprietress drifted back to the bar to complete their order, he turned again to the Elder. "Okay, you need a new line. 'Black, the way God drinks it.' I've lost track of the number of times you've used that one."

The Elder affected an air of indulgent patience. "Well, I *was* a teacher at one point, and repetition is so vital to the learning process. And since you still insist on poisoning your coffee with 'all the fixings', my work is clearly not finished. And I trust you took note of the cause-and-effect of my cutlery placement?"

"Noted," snorted the Younger. "Now, could you drop the smug look?"

The Elder laughed out loud; it was a golden sound, the rich enjoyment of friendship and conversation overflowing into a spontaneous expression. "If 'pride goeth before a fall', does that mean I'll have you to thank for tripping me? Or am I responsible for my own demise?"

The Younger, unable to keep a straight face, joined in his merriment, even as the Proprietress returned at precisely that moment with their steaming mugs of coffee. And, as requested, a tiny metal pitcher filled with cream, flanked by a collection of refined sugar, raw sugar, and various brightly packaged sugar substitutes.

Their laughter appeared to relax the Proprietress, as she set down their drinks and the accompanying 'fixings'. There was even a slight hint of her own smile as she tucked the serving tray under her arm and bustled back to the bar.

"I think she's getting over the meat cleaver," suggested the Younger, lowering his voice, just in case. "Which reminds me: Did you have anything to add to the pragmatic side of our discussion on the apocalyptics?"

"Well, the *real* meat of the matter," suggested the Elder, nudging the cleaver under its concealing cover and pretending not to notice the Younger's pained expression at his weak pun, "will come when we look at Jesus' teaching about the Kingdom, of course. But if I were to look at the apocalyptics a certain way, I would encourage us to add a healthier, more robust *eschatological* flavor to our theological stew. Without adopting an 'it's all gonna burn' extreme, of course."

Seeing the quizzical look on the Younger face, and anticipating the coming question, he continued, "The apocalyptics lived their lives with the hope for a better future, one where the Kingdom of God would become *the* defining reality of the world. I know you're looking for a practical, hands-on, pragmatic application, but I'd like to suggest that a healthy view of the coming Kingdom *in the future* must inform the manner in which we live in the here-and-now. That's why I am convinced that *eschatology* – the doctrine of the end times – is important today."

A look of dawning comprehension spread across the Younger's face, even as he added cream and sugar to his coffee, stirring vigorously. "Right, because we don't bring the Kingdom, only Jesus does. And that means we don't know *when* it will come, which can't help but change the way we view life in the present."

Lifting his steaming mug of coffee, the Elder inhaled deeply of its dusky aroma, and concluded: "Call it 'pragmatism in light of the future', or 'a theology of hope', if you will. But I think it would, or at least, it *should*, greatly impact our daily lives, if we were to keep the future, apocalyptic coming of the Kingdom in mind."

"True, that," agreed the Younger, lifting his own mug of coffee in salute.

The Elder drank deeply, and then casually reached into the selection of condiments on their table, selecting a bottle of ketchup. With a sly smile and a knowing look, he held the bottle up between them.

But this time, however, neither the Barkeep nor the Proprietress appeared in the least bit concerned.

Thor's Hammer Notes

1. *The Presence of the Future*, 89
2. Ibid., 94
3. Ibid., 95-96
4. Ibid., 97

Further Conversations

1. There are many historical examples of God working through people: William Wilberforce, William Booth (co-founder of the Salvation Army), Mother Theresa, Martin Luther, Martin Luther King Jr., St. Francis of Assisi. All of these people had an impact on the justice issues of their day because of their faith. Use Google or Wikipedia as a starting place to learn more about one or more of them.

2. Read some of the Biblical passages about the Day of the Lord. For example: Isaiah 2:12-22, Joel 2:28-32, and Malachi 4:1-6 *(the last words in the Old Testament)*. How would you describe the *Day of the Lord* in your own words for our current context?

3. Based on the previous question, does the *Day of the Lord* sound like 'good news'? For whom? What kind of people will *not* be happy to see the Kingdom come in its fullness?

4. Agree/disagree: Any genuine move of God will always be met with violent opposition.

<u>Extra credit:</u>

1. As a group, watch the video "Amazing Grace" about the dismantling of the slave trade, and discuss.

2. Read anything by Henri Nouwen, or listen to interviews with Mother Theresa of Calcutta.

chapter Six
salsa picante

The Younger began to laugh once more. “You wouldn’t know the meaning of the word ‘subtle’ if somebody painted the definition on every billboard in town, would you?”

The Elder chuckled as he placed the ketchup bottle, with exaggerated care and significance, in the precise middle of the table, equidistant between the Younger and himself. Looking up from his meticulous ceremony of placement, he locked eyes with the Younger, an inscrutable expression on his craggy face.

“Okay, you win,” conceded the Younger, after what seemed a small eternity, although it couldn’t have truly lasted more than a few seconds. Schooling himself to maintain the same neutral expression as the Elder, he shrugged and asked, “Am I to assume you’re ready to move on to the third and final act of our drama-in-three-parts?”

The Elder’s poker face dissolved into his usual open demeanor, as he looked down with a smile at his weathered copy of Ladd's book. "Well, let's put it this way: the sun was up when we arrived, and I really have no desire to prop myself up with caffeine for the rest of the evening. I would no doubt find myself lying awake in bed all night, counting spots on my ceiling."

The Younger looked out the window to his right, surprised to see that the Elder's observation about the passage of time was undeniably accurate. The trees in the park across the road were now shrouded in darkness, as the street-lamps bathed the intervening sidewalks and asphalt in a warm glow.

"Wow, you're not kidding. We'd better pick up the pace a little, eh?" he remarked, turning back to face the Elder and drawing his own digital copy of Ladd a little closer. "The saltshaker was about ethics, and the meat cleaver was about the Kingdom breaking into history like the Hammer of Thor, and the salsa picante, or ketchup, is what again?"

"The Rule and Reign of God," intoned the Elder in his best radio announcer's voice, accentuating each word for greater emphasis.

"And specifically, the whole notion of 'kingdoms in conflict', which also runs throughout and underneath the saltshaker school of thought, as well as the apocalyptic.

"They may have had different understandings about how and why the Kingdom would come, but they were all in agreement on this point. The Kingdom was all about the rule and reign of God, the King of heaven and earth."

The Younger nodded in recognition, quickly flipping a few digital pages. "Let's see if I can impress you with some Greek and Hebrew," he said with a smile. "Listen to this:

> "The majority of exegetes have recognized that the central meaning of basileia, as of the Hebrew word malkuth, is the abstract or dynamic idea of reign, rule, or dominion rather than the concrete idea of realm."[1]

Before the Elder could respond, the Younger answered the question that he knew, from long experience, would follow. "Yes, I admit: I didn't really read the Greek and Hebrew. I'm just quoting Ladd, and trusting that he's an honest writer."

The Elder smiled but said nothing. They were both well aware of his pet peeve regarding people who didn't do their own research, but blindly accepted whatever they were told. "Being a critical thinker isn't a negative thing", he was known to insist, to whomever would listen, "unless you're a negative person to begin with." But on this occasion, he let it slide (just this once).

"The word that we translate as 'kingdom' in the New Testament," the Younger continued, "is the Greek word *basileia*, which has the same meaning as the Old Testament Hebrew word *malkuth*. And Ladd is pointing out that the generally agreed-upon understanding of *basileia* is not about a geographical area. It's about God's authority to rule, period. His sovereignty."

The Elder lifted his coffee mug in salute. "That's a very important distinction for those of us who don't have Jewish ethnicity, isn't it? The Kingdom as the 'rule and reign of God' is not limited to one nation but can, and does, exist everywhere. This is one of those times where Jesus expands, or re-directs, their expectations. They would have assumed that the 'kingdom' meant their country, but it was much more than that."

The Elder paused momentarily, as he dared to beckon to the Proprietress for more coffee. "It's important to note that the 'kingdoms in conflict' understanding runs throughout Israel's history. For example, in the book of Exodus, we read about the conflict between Pharaoh and Yahweh. Not only were the Israelites freed from slavery, but also all the 'gods' of the ancient Egyptians were defeated through the Ten Plagues. By the time the Israelites arrived at Mount Sinai, they had had quite a few dramatic proofs that God was the ultimate King. Or, as we used to say, 'God Almighty', the peerless One."

The Proprietress swept by their table, as the pub's patrons gradually dwindled in number with the waning evening. (Which is why the two of them came to the pub on Monday evenings; the weekend atmosphere was a different thing entirely.)

Wordlessly, she deftly refilled each of their proffered coffee mugs, before stepping back a pace or two to point out that, unlike other, less-worthy eateries, their coffee was always fresh, and would never be served by leaving a lukewarm carafe on their table.

She was gone before either of them could say anything. They looked at each other for a moment, eyebrows raised, and then by unspoken consent, promptly returned to their books and conversation.

"The fascinating thing for me," enthused the Younger, as he stirred the freshly mixed fixings in his coffee, "is that during Old Testament times, it was actual human kingdoms in conflict with God's kingdom. But when Jesus began his public ministry, His main conflict, aside from the religious leaders, was with the power *behind* the worldly kingdoms: Satan himself." Holding his coffee in one hand, and the e-reader in the other, he announced:

> "The Kingdom is God's dynamic power, and it must 'come' because there are real spiritual enemies which oppose it, both human and super-human. The 'coming' of God's Kingdom means the invasion of the power of Satan and the overthrow of his kingdom."[2]

The Younger continued reading, blissfully unaware that his natural enthusiasm was threatening to spill hot coffee over the rim of his cup. The Elder held his breath, hoping for the best.

> "The victory over demons is a victory in the spiritual realm; but it took place because Jesus came on the plane of history to overthrow evil and deliver men from bondage."[3]

Setting his reader down and draining half of his coffee in a single, scorching (and regrettable) gulp, the Younger sputtered briefly, and yet somehow managed to stay on topic with barely a pause.

"It reminds me of the scene in that old Wizard of Oz movie, when the curtain is removed, and the real source of the fearsome Wizard was revealed to just be a puny little man with a lot of special effects." He looked up momentarily, as another thought occurred to him. "Except that in the New Testament, what is revealed is not a mere mortal trying to appear bigger than he is, but an evil spiritual being pulling the strings behind the scenes."

The Elder saluted him with his coffee mug a second time. "And it's perhaps of some significance that when Jesus announced the Kingdom's arrival, He didn't go after Rome as everyone expected. Instead, He went after the spiritual powers *behind* the political and societal powers."

The Younger paused for a long moment, as the implications of the Elder's words sank in. "Okay, you've just messed with my mind, big time," he managed finally. "It never occurred to me to associate the issues of justice with spiritual warfare before. I'm going to have to do some thinking on that one."

The Elder couldn't help but tease him a little. "Really? I've left you speechless and without retort? It must be the lateness of the hour."

Finishing the remainder of his coffee, the Elder set the mug aside and gave his full attention to the dog-eared pages before him. "What is clear, I believe, is that Jesus certainly understood that His mission of proclaiming the Kingdom of

God was an assault on the kingdom of this world, and on the power behind it. The 'kingdoms in conflict' was no longer between nations, but between God and the usurper, the devil, or Satan."

Scanning through his bookmarks, he found the quote he was looking for and read:

> "The ultimate coming of God's Kingdom and the universal establishment of his reign will mean nothing less than the destruction of the very principle of evil in the spiritual realm..."

The Elder skipped a little further down the same page, running his finger along the written lines as he continued.

> "This victory over Satan is the same whether it be described as a binding of the strong man (Matthew) or stripping him of his armor (Luke). In metaphorical language Jesus interprets his own mission among men as an invasion of Satan's kingdom (Matthew 12:26) for the purpose of assaulting the Evil One, overcoming him, and despoiling him of his goods."[4]

"This time, it's personal," quipped the Younger, thoughtfully, as the implications began to sink in.

"It looks like Jesus is taking this to a whole other level and intensifying the conflict. I guess that makes sense, since He's preaching 'the Kingdom is near'. Jesus provokes a strong reaction from the demons, because He is on the offensive, and so that puts them on the defensive."

"First epistle of John, chapter three, verse eight," agreed the Elder. "'The reason the Son of God appeared was to destroy the devil's work.'"[5]

"But why wouldn't Jesus let the demons say He was the Son of God?" wondered the Younger, perplexed. "It was probably the only time they actually told the truth."

The Elder laughed. "Don't be so sure it was the only time; the most effective deceptions always contain just enough truth to seduce people. But remember the expectations of the people for a political messiah? A messiah who would free them from Rome and restore Israel to the good old days of King David?"

"Jesus' choice to silence the demons might be partly to do with not wanting His Messiahship announced by evil spirits. How would that look, having demons doing your P.R.?" They both enjoyed a chuckle at the thought.

"But it's also likely," the Elder went on, "that Jesus was simply avoiding the trap of peoples' expectations. They actually wanted to force Him to be king, at one point, but He escaped. He preferred to refer to Himself as the 'Son of Man', another Old Testament term that couples quite nicely with the concept of the Suffering Servant."

The Younger snapped his fingers. "Yes, I remember that one. It fits right in with Jesus rewriting their expectations, doesn't it? They were expecting a conquering political savior, and instead – was it in Matthew's gospel? –they got a messiah who came 'riding on a donkey'."

"Yes, it was Matthew[6], quoting a prophecy from Zechariah[7]," confirmed the Elder. "The key here, though, is that Jesus was announcing that the Kingdom was *very, very near* – already present, in fact – but not as they'd expected." Turning to the most prominent bookmark in his copy, he read:

> "God's Kingdom, his reign, will come at the end of the age in a mighty irruption into history inaugurating the perfect order of the age to come. But God's Kingdom, his reign has already come into history in the person and mission of Jesus."[8]

The Younger finished the remaining coffee in his mug, now much cooler than the scorching gulp he'd foolishly taken earlier, and set his mug aside as the Elder had done. "That is one of the most amazing things that I read, to be honest. The idea that the Kingdom has already come in Jesus, even though it won't completely be here until sometime in the future. After reading Ladd, now I can understand what your theological friends mean when they talk about the 'already and not yet' Kingdom."

The Elder's face crinkled around his eyes as a pleased smile spread across his face. "I'll remember to tell them of your newfound appreciation of the term. Although, sadly, it appears the kitchen is now closed for the night," he observed, watching several additional workers stack chairs on top of tables they'd just cleaned. "It also looks as though they're not brewing fresh coffee anymore, either."

A quick survey of the bar's interior revealed that they were among the few remaining patrons in the pub. The Barkeep was still polishing the counter, more out of habit than need by this time in the evening.

The Younger stretched, stifling a yawn. "I guess we should take that as a hint to wrap things up, eh?"

The Elder turned back to face him, leaning forward with intentness. "That's a pity. We've just now arrived at the key, the lynchpin, if you like, of Ladd's understanding of the 'already and not yet' nature of the Kingdom. This background understanding will be absolutely priceless as we start exploring what Jesus taught about the Kingdom. I'll concede that this as good a place as any to wind up our discussion this evening, but I would be remiss to not mention just one more thing."

"You may have noticed this particular bookmark," continued the Elder, taking hold of it between his thumb and forefinger, "which is the largest and most prominent by design. Listen to what Ladd says here:

> "This brings us to our central thesis: that before the eschatological appearing of God's Kingdom at the end of the age, God's Kingdom has become dynamically active among men in Jesus' person and mission.
>
> "The Kingdom in this age is not merely the abstract concept of God's universal rule to which men must submit; it is rather a dynamic power at work among men."[9]

The Younger leaned forward, his chin a scant twelve inches above the surface of the table. "The first thing that comes to mind, pragmatically speaking of course, is that passivity is not an option. I mean, the apocalyptics were expecting the Kingdom to come with a big bang, and they were basically just killing time, waiting to be rescued. But if the Kingdom is 'dynamic' – active in the real world – then you can't just sit there, passively. You have to respond to it, one way or the other."

He leaned back, eyes fixed on the Elder's book across the table, as he mentally connected the dots. "Okay, so on one hand, we don't bring the Kingdom; only God does. On the other hand, the activity of the Kingdom means that we have to respond, in some way."

It was as if a light had been switched on somewhere. The Younger eagerly flipped through a few more pages in his digital copy, before announcing with satisfaction, "Ah, here it is. Get this:

> "The rabbis taught that men should take upon them the yoke of the Kingdom and accept the law as the norm of God's will. Jesus taught that because God has acted, because the dynamic power of his Kingdom has invaded the world, men are to respond with a radical reaction."[10]

The Elder nodded in agreement. "The 'God who comes'," he said quietly, elbows on the table, fingers steepled. "It's in keeping with the entire history of the Israelites, really. God comes, and they are faced with a choice of how they will respond. Will they be with Him, or not? That was the choice Moses gave them after the incident with the golden calf, as we discussed before. Elijah on Mount Carmel, and so on. *No-one would have been shocked, in the first century, that Jesus' announcement of the Kingdom would require a decision from them.*"

The Younger continued to scan the page before him. Holding up the reader once more, he exclaimed, "Yes, I see what you mean. Ladd words it even more strongly here:

> **"Men cannot passively await the coming of the eschatological Kingdom as the apocalyptists taught. On the contrary, the Kingdom has come to them, and they are actively, aggressively, forcefully to seize it."[11]**

Lowering the reader to the table again, the Younger had another thought. "Really, you could say it's all about allegiance, couldn't you? There are two kingdoms in conflict, and 'repenting' in order to receive the Kingdom is all about changing where your allegiance lies, first and foremost. You're changing sides."

"And your actions in the Kingdom would be the 'fruit' of that allegiance," agreed the Elder, warming instantly to the Younger's metaphor. "It stands completely opposite to the prophetic school of thought. That's why John the Baptist was considered one of the last of the prophets: he was preaching a baptism of repentance in order to be ready for the Kingdom. And shortly thereafter, Jesus inaugurated a new era, in which your behavior changes as a result of the Kingdom coming to you."

The Younger grinned and held his head in his hands. "My brain is going to explode! Just as you said that, a whole list of New Testament verses came to mind. Again, the practical implications..." his voice trailed off.

Just then, they both realized that the lights in other sections of the pub were being extinguished. Recognizing, however belatedly, that the hints being given about the posted hours of operation were becoming less subtle, they stood up and began to put on their coats.

"Any final thoughts? Questions? More quotations?" teased the Elder, as he tugged the ends of his sleeves into place and buttoned his jacket.

"Just the obvious," chided the Younger with a knowing smile. "Don't forget your meat cleaver."

The Elder laughed, and with an exaggerated conspiratorial air, deftly scooped up the offensive utensil, wrapping the oilcloth around it and stowing it in his satchel. "Thank you for the reminder. I would hate to be the cause of more drama, just as we were leaving."

"The other thought that comes to mind," continued the Younger, as if he hadn't heard his friend's comment, "has to do with how the Kingdom moves forward today. For example, if it's still true that we don't bring the Kingdom, only God does, then what's our role? Beyond responding personally, I mean?"

He shoved his electronics back into his messenger bag as the two of them headed for the exit: not the last patrons to leave, but almost. "We'll get to explore that, and much more, at a later date," promised the Elder, reaching for the heavy wooden front door. "For tonight, I think our best take-away is understanding the 'kingdoms in conflict' motif, as well as the idea that the Kingdom is both already here, and yet still in the future."

The door swung shut behind them, and the Elder fumbled with his weathered book, holding it up to the streetlamp nearest them for better illumination. "I'll leave you with this final thought from Ladd," he said, squinting at the text.

> "In some real sense of the word, the Kingdom is itself present. It is not merely the signs of the Kingdom or the powers of the Kingdom, but the Kingdom itself which is said to be present."[12]

Looking up at his younger friend, the Elder spread his arms wide, indicating the area all around them. "So, even here in this place, on this street, at this time of night, I can say with confidence: 'the Kingdom is near'. It wasn't withdrawn when Jesus ascended back to heaven, was it? The whole book of Acts – actually, the rest of the entire New Testament – shows that the Kingdom didn't leave with Jesus. It is here, right now, forcefully advancing."

"'And the forceful ones lay hold of it'. Matthew eleven, verse twelve," remembered the Younger, feeling goose bumps rise on the back of his neck as a mild breeze ruffled his hair. Looking around in the stillness of the night, the diffused glow of the street-lamps giving the entire scene a surreal quality, he caught the briefest of glimpses that come from seeing the world with new eyes.

"I feel like I'm in *The Matrix*, and everything I thought I knew, looks different somehow," he said finally, wondering if the other would understand.

"Does that make me Morpheus?" queried the Elder innocently, smiling at the surprised expression on the Younger's face.

The Elder closed his book with a muffled snap, as if that settled everything, and stuffed it back into his satchel. By unspoken mutual consent, the two friends began the trek towards their parked cars, a mere half block away. "Well, anyway," concluded the Younger, "I just meant that if I could somehow remember 'the kingdom is near', no matter where I am or what I'm doing, like I'm aware right now, it could revolutionize my whole life."

"And the forceful ones lay hold of it," agreed the Elder under his breath, as he did his best to keep up with his friend's longer strides.

Salsa Picante Notes

1. *The Presence of the Future*, 130
    - *Basileia*: royal power, kingship, dominion, rule; not to be confused with an actual kingdom but rather the right or authority to rule over a kingdom; of the royal power of Jesus as the triumphant Messiah
    - *Malkuth:* royal power, dominion, reign, kingdom, realm
2. Ibid., 155
3. Ibid., 156
4. Ibid., 151
5. 1 John 3:8
6. Matthew 21:1-11; specific quote is 21:5
7. Zechariah 9:9
8. *The Presence of the Future*, 144
9. Ibid., 139
10. Ibid., 163
11. Ibid., 164
12. Ibid., 143

Further Conversations

Reminder: Are the three symbols on your table?

1. Agree/Disagree: The word Satan simply means: "to obstruct, or to oppose", and therefore only refers to people or situations that oppose you (rather than an actual malevolent spiritual being).
2. If dark spiritual beings are behind societal injustice, how do we fight them? How does your view of dealing with injustice change?
3. There is a lot of expectation in some church circles that we can see the modern-day restoration of "David's Tabernacle" – a sort of 'golden age' that has been lost. This is remarkably similar to Israel's expectation for the first coming of Jesus. How might such an expectation affect our actions and focus?
4. Have you seen evidence that the Kingdom of God is hear already and yet still coming? Not stories from somewhere on the Internet or from someone whose cousin's neighbor's former hairdresser's dog's owner that may or may not be totally accurate... what have *you* seen? Tell each other these stories!
5. What image comes to mind when you hear the phrase: 'the Kingdom is near'?

Extra Credit:

1. Read, meditate on, and discuss together Matthew 21.

chapter Seven
enter jesus

The pleasant aroma of espresso and a variety of baked goods wafted over me as I pulled the heavy wooden door open and entered the coffee shop. The overlapping of multiple conversations produced a lively murmur, which was in its own way as familiar and welcoming as the sights and smells.

As the door swung shut behind me with a soft and heavy whoosh, I remained where I was for an additional moment, basking in the familiar ethos.

This is why I love the Genesis Café, I thought to myself.

En route to the espresso bar, I glanced instinctively to my right, wondering if the raised window seats at the front of the building were available. I was rewarded with the discovery that our favorite perch was indeed vacant, and I quickened my pace towards the espresso bar. *This will be the fastest order-and-pay of all time,* I thought to myself, eager to claim the coveted seats.

The Barista, whom I recognized but whose name I could never recall, was clad as always completely in black, with enough visible piercings in her ears and face to give airport security fits. She was usually pleasant but a little reserved, but this afternoon, she looked as if she might explode with excitement. Or perhaps she'd sampled the espresso more often than usual.

"How are you doing today?" I asked absent-mindedly, with only the briefest moment of eye contact. I was already reading the drink board behind her, my thoughts consumed with getting that window seat.

"I'm doing *great*", she enthused loudly, with an even wider smile, if that were possible. "I just had *the* most amazing thing happen today! It totally blew my mind!"

The drink board and my mission of reserving the window seats evaporated like mist on a sunny morning, as she had now captured my complete attention. Before I could ask the obvious question, she gushed on.

"I always take off my engagement ring when I'm cleaning the inside of the espresso machine, just because it's so *ridiculously* hard to get coffee grounds out of all the nooks and crannies in my ring." She held up her left hand as she spoke, waving it from side to side with such enthusiasm that the ring was a glinting blur, as was the rest of her hand.

"But today, I was cleaning like normal: you know, early in the shift, before we open our doors, but when I was done, I couldn't find the ring *anywhere*. And so I was totally freaking out, and looking everywhere. I mean, under the fridges, behind the cash register – I was practically bawling because, like what if I'd lost it forever?"

I could only stand there, nodding with a sympathetic smile on my face as she raced on. *How does she talk without stopping for a breath?* I wondered.

"But then, *there it was!*" She trilled, bouncing up on her toes momentarily, pointing between the many bottles of syrup beside the espresso machine. "I guess I put it on top of one of the bottles, and it fell between them or something. And I was so relieved, that's when I *totally* started crying." She finally stopped to catch her breath, eyes beginning to fill with tears once more, in sharp contrast to her neon-bright smile.

Her happiness was so contagious that I was probably smiling as widely as she was. You would have to be pretty cold-hearted not to identify with her sense of relief at finding her ring. Remembering what I'd come for (and mindful of the line-up behind me), I congratulated her on her good fortune, and ordered my latte.

Cup in hand, I turned towards the front of the coffee shop, only to spot someone casually sifting through the local newspaper at *my* window seat. Sighing, I looked around the rest of the shop and chose one of the few remaining tables against the far wall. It was still a window seat, technically. But instead of the tree-lined street, the only view offered by the much smaller window was of the neighboring building's brickwork, so close it was almost within touching distance.

While I waited, I pulled my denim-covered journal out of my briefcase, and began pouring over the notes I'd made during my readings in the Gospels. Not surprisingly, I had experienced a growing sense of excitement when I'd read through Jesus' teaching on the Kingdom. At the same time, there had been a few items that were thought provoking, especially in Matthew's Gospel, and I was looking forward to bouncing ideas around with my co-conspirators.

As if on cue, the Younger and the Elder chose that moment to burst through the door of the café. It didn't seem to matter what time we agreed on, I was almost always the first to arrive. *I'll bet it's got something to do with the Elder trying to dock his land yacht*, I thought, as the two of them waved at me, en route to ordering their own drinks. While they were busy, I continued to go over my notes, particularly the lists I'd made as I went through the gospel of Matthew.

I was so absorbed in what I was reading that their sudden arrival at the table, drinks in hand, startled me. The two of them were laughing quietly to themselves as they grabbed their seats, the Younger beside me, and the Elder seating himself across the table, facing both of us.

"Come now," the Elder was saying to the Younger, "haven't you ever lost something valuable and then found it again, once you'd almost given up hope? You would be as over-joyed as our young barista, I'd imagine."

"I'm not arguing with you," protested the Younger, although both his grin and his eyes proclaimed that it was only a mild protest. "I was just observing that she's not normally that excitable when we come in here, that's all."

The Elder looked at me. "Someday, he'll understand," he commented with a smile, shaking his head in mock exasperation. "Personally, I will always choose to 'rejoice with those who rejoice'."

The Younger was already moving on, eagerly pulling the e-reader out of his messenger bag and tapping the screen into vibrant life. "I'm glad she found her ring," he said absently, as his eyes scanned through several pages in his e-book. "I was only commenting on how she's telling the same story to every customer who comes in, over and over again."

"It's a good story, and she tells it well," I agreed, sipping my latte before it cooled. "And her enthusiasm *is* pretty contagious," I had to admit, in reference to the Elder's earlier comment. He nodded with a smile.

"Ah, here it is," announced the Younger triumphantly, holding his e-reader up as a prelude to reading.

The Elder sipped cautiously at his coffee, directing his comment to me. "He's been talking about this 'new wrinkle' on the Kingdom of God ever since I picked him up at his office, twenty minutes ago. I doubt we'll get much further until we talk about it."

I sat up a little straighter, readying myself for our usual spirited dialogue. "Okay, then let's have at it, shall we? Oh, by the way," I addressed the Younger, "thanks for sending me all those emails about the saltshaker, the salsa, and the notorious meat-cleaver-in-the-pub episode."

The reminder of their misadventures caused the two of them to erupt in a healthy burst of laughter, although not quite as loud or as animated as the barista with her found-again engagement ring. "I'm pleased to hear you enjoyed yourself – at our expense," the Elder replied with a note of rebuke in his voice, reliving the moment in his mind.

"I like the metaphors you two were developing," I replied, paying my respects with what remained of my latte, before downing the last of it. "I'm a visual learner, so I appreciate using real-life objects as symbols." Keeping a straight face, I managed to successfully (but barely) resist the temptation to add any further comments about their adventures with the cleaver.

Pointing at the Elder with his e-reader, the Younger pulled us back on topic. "At least *I* wrote a summary on what we talked about," he replied. "After all, we spent an entire evening on it."

"Okay, okay," the Elder conceded with a good-natured chuckle, "and here I thought you just wanted to show off all the marvels your electronic gizmo can do."

"*Ahem*," began the Younger, clearing his throat for emphasis as he began to read the quote that had captured his attention.

> "The Kingdom of God has come into the world to be received by some but rejected by others. The Kingdom is in the present to have only partial

> **success, and this success is dependent upon a human response."[1]**

"I'm not saying I think Ladd has totally missed it," he began cautiously, setting his reader down on the table, "but if you want to have an unpopular opinion in this day and age, try telling people that not everyone inherits the Kingdom. It sounds... well, almost like *blasphemy*, to suggest that the Kingdom could 'fail', simply based on how people respond to it. Or don't respond."

The Elder nodded thoughtfully, gazing at a spot just over our shoulders, the way he often did when choosing his words carefully before speaking. Taking advantage of his momentary silence, I turned to the Younger. "Funny you should bring that up today," I said, indicating my journal, with the notes on Matthew I had just been reviewing, "because I was going to bring up an interesting pattern in Jesus' teaching about the Kingdom being near."

The Elder interposed at that moment, gently but firmly covering the pages of my journal with his hand, the simple gesture commanding our attention. "I would like to suggest that we would be wise to follow Ladd's exhortation on *how* we approach this topic."

He smiled a little as he continued, no doubt recognizing the uncomprehending expressions on our faces. "My advantage is that I've been around long enough to have read a great deal of Ladd's work, and there is a quote from one of his earliest publications that I think speaks to this moment. If I may?"

Continuing to cover my journal with one hand, the Elder opened his battered copy of *Jesus and the Kingdom* with his other hand, looking at one of the blank pages inside the front cover. From my vantage point across the table, I marveled at the remarkably neat cursive writing, in the Elder's own hand, of the quote that he wanted to share with us.

> **"This problem must not be solved by abstract theological reasoning but by the exegesis of the Scriptures. The point of departure must always be, 'What do the Scriptures teach?' rather than, 'What does logic allow'?"[2]**

The Elder raised his eyes, looking back and forth at the Younger and me. "Ladd wrote that in 1952, and it was – and is – such a wise observation, that I jotted it down for future reference. I knew it was inevitable that the two of you would need to hear it at some point," he smiled gently as he looked to the Younger.

"We *could* debate the quote from Ladd which you just read from a philosophical perspective, of course. But I think we would be wisest to follow Ladd's own approach: what do the Scriptures say? Including," and now he removed his hand from my journal, drawing our attention back to its scribbled pages, "whatever it is you've found in Matthew's gospel."

The Younger looked at me with mischievous resignation. "He knows us too well, doesn't he?" Nodding in agreement, I picked up the journal and flipped a few pages, eager to pick up on my earlier thought.

"When I'm researching a topic in the Bible, I usually begin by reading the whole gospel at one sitting, just to get familiar with the flow. And I noticed something significant about many of the times Jesus talked about the Kingdom, especially when He was using parables to explain it."

I paused for a moment, taking a deep breath before plunging on. "To put it bluntly, Jesus taught that *how* people responded to His message would determine whether or not they'd inherit the Kingdom." Turning towards the Younger, I hastened to add, "And I agree with you: that's not a popular opinion these days."

"This was part of our *salsa picante* discussion, if you recall," the Elder remarked, also directing his comment to the Younger. "The 'God who comes' has now come in the person of Jesus, and brought a full frontal assault on the kingdom of Satan. Throughout the Old Testament, we can trace this theme of God coming, and the people being given a choice: how will they respond? The golden calf incident[3]. Joshua renewing the covenant with the whole nation[4]. Elijah's ultimatum: serve Baal or serve God[5]."

The Elder reached down beside his chair, fumbling with his old leather satchel, and brought out a large Bible that was even more dog-eared and battered than his copy of Ladd. Flipping it open, the Elder looked back at us. "Who speaks the first reference to the Kingdom in Matthew? Actually, it's not Jesus at all. It's John the Baptist, preparing the way, in chapter three. But he introduces the same challenge as any Old Testament prophet: a choice must be made, and that choice has serious implications.

Listen to John the Baptist's words to the Pharisees who came to observe his baptisms. It's fiery stuff."

"You brood of vipers! Who warned you to flee from the coming wrath? Produce fruit in keeping with repentance. And do not think you can say to yourselves, 'We have Abraham as our father.' I tell you that out of these stones God can raise up children for Abraham. The axe is already at the root of the trees, and every tree that does not produce good fruit will be cut down and thrown into the fire. I baptize you with water for repentance. But after me will come one who is more powerful than I, whose sandals I am not fit to carry. He will baptize you with the Holy Spirit and with fire. His winnowing fork is in his hand, and he will clear his threshing floor, gathering his wheat into the barn and burning up the chaff with unquenchable fire."[6]

The Younger stirred in his chair as a new thought occurred to him. "I remember that Ladd had an interesting take on the meaning of Jesus baptizing 'with the Holy Spirit and with fire'. Remember, I come from a charismatic background, and some of the speakers I heard in our church made it sound like 'fire' was another reference to being baptized by the Spirit. But Ladd's opinion was that fire was judgment, not blessing."

"It fits the context of Matthew three, and John the Baptist's words about separating the wheat from the chaff," the Elder quietly concurred, not wanting to get drawn into a rabbit trail. "What I had hoped to point out was the consistency with the Old Testament idea of a 'remnant': simply being a descendant of Abraham was not enough, and participation in the coming Kingdom would require a response of some kind."

I was listening intently, my journal notes momentarily forgotten. "I've heard some people argue that John talked that way because he was the last of the Old Testament-style prophets," I suggested. "And because Jesus had now arrived, John's words no longer apply."

Gesturing towards the Elder's Bible, I hastening to complete my thought. "Except that it's clear throughout Matthew, and Luke and John, that Jesus also spoke a great deal about the coming separation. He used metaphors like separating wheat from weeds[7], good fish from bad fish[8], and sheep from goats[9] to describe what would happen when the Kingdom would come. That's what I was referring to earlier: there's a definite pattern in how Jesus speaks about the Kingdom."

From the inside pocket of my journal cover, I retrieved the folded lists that I'd printed earlier that afternoon, in anticipation of our time together. "Here's all the biblical references to Jesus speaking about separating people into two groups when the Kingdom finally comes in its fullness. There are so many examples that I thought it would be helpful to write all the references down. And it's not just Matthew, as you can see, it's also in Luke and John, too." *(See Appendix: Teaching of Jesus on the Coming Separation)*

"I wonder why not in Mark," mused the Younger, frowning at his copy of the list. "Wasn't Mark's gospel written first, and didn't Matthew and Luke use it as a resource when they wrote their own gospels?"

The Elder quietly perused his own copy of the list, as I responded to the Younger's comment. "I was wondering why Matthew made such a big deal of it, too, until I remembered who Matthew wrote his gospel to: his own people, the Jews. That's why there's so many verses that start with 'this was to fulfill', followed by an Old Testament prophecy. Matthew was writing to convince his fellow Jews that Jesus *was* the promised Messiah, even if He came in a way that they weren't expecting."

The Elder lowered his copy of the list to the table as he added, "And Luke was writing to a Gentile friend of his, by the name of Theophilus, but he stresses the same things as Matthew. We must avoid the mistake of assuming the separation dynamic only applied to Israel and their acceptance or rejection of the Messiah. The Kingdom *always* asks that people respond."

"And the forceful ones lay hold of it," murmured the Younger, still studying his list, as with his other hand, he opened a Bible program on his reader.

"And Mark's gospel *does* include some references to a coming separation[10], although not as clearly or as often as in the other Gospels," the Elder continued, firmly but gently, now looking at me. "What comes across much stronger as a theme in Mark is: (a) the sheer number of times where demons are cast out, and (b) the many stories of Jesus' miracles. You can't miss the 'kingdoms in conflict' dynamic when reading Mark."

"Yet you *missed* the verses about the Kingdom in Mark?" gasped the Younger in mock horror, eyebrows raised. He leaned as far away from me as he could, without tipping himself out of his chair. "I'd better not sit too close to you. I wouldn't want to get toasted if and when the lightning bolt strikes!"

I had to laugh, although I'm sure my embarrassment was on display for all to see, despite the gracious way in which the Elder had pointed out my oversight.

"Well," I managed at last, "I guess the good news is that we can confidently say that *all* the Gospels include an understanding that there is a coming separation when the Kingdom arrives."

"Good save," winked the Younger, unwilling to allow the opportunity to have some fun at my expense slide away too quickly.

Before I could formulate a clever retort, the Elder coughed politely and quietly into his hand, like a professor drawing the attention of squabbling students back to where it belonged.

"This 'separation dynamic' will come up very strongly again, once we're looking at the Parables of the Kingdom," he suggested, once he could see that we were listening.

"But before we go any further, I want to revisit something that we must keep in mind as we move forward."

Setting aside his copy of the list, he turned a few pages to another book-marked passage in his copy of Ladd. Adjusting his reading glasses slightly, he cleared his throat and read:

> "The present aspect of the Kingdom neither replaces nor reinterprets the eschatological aspect; rather it supplements it.
>
> "The same God who will manifest his Kingdom at the end of history in apocalyptic glory is now exercising that same kingly power in the person of Jesus to carry forward his redemptive purposes within history."[11]

Removing his glasses, he gestured expansively with his hands as he continued. "We've probably said more than enough about the 'already and not yet' aspect of the Kingdom, but always keep it in the back of your minds. Jesus is announcing that the Kingdom *has come* – present tense – in *Him*. He is the King, and therefore, it is He who brings the Kingdom."

"But, let's also bear in mind," the Elder shifted in his chair, using his reading glasses almost as a pointer as he spoke, "that a response was required from the people who heard His message, because the Kingdom had come *within history*, even though it will also later come apocalyptically. The 'big bang', as my young friend so eloquently called it."

"So, if Jesus embodies the Kingdom," suggested the Younger slowly, frowning in thought, "then would it be reasonable to say that accepting Jesus is the same as accepting the Kingdom?"

"*Entering* the Kingdom," corrected the Elder, as gently as he had done earlier with me. "Remember, we receive the Kingdom as a gift; we don't earn it by our own efforts. And conversely, rejecting Jesus means rejecting God's Kingly rule. Jesus isn't the Kingdom, He is the King of it. When we surrender to His rule and reign, we enter the Kingdom."

The Younger started forward suddenly in his seat, eyes glued to the screen of his reader. "Wow, I was just about to quote the most famous Bible verse in the world, thanks to all those guys with the John 3:16 signs at sporting events, and I realized that I almost missed something. Listen to this, you guys:

"For God so loved the world that he gave his one and only Son, that whoever believes in him shall not perish but have eternal life. For God did not send his Son into the world to condemn the world, but to save the world through him. Whoever believes in him is not condemned, but whoever does not believe stands condemned already because he has not believed in the name of God's one and only Son."[12]

The Younger looked up, shaking his head in wonderment. "I was about to quote the part about Jesus coming to save, not to condemn. But then I read the next verse." He leaned back in his chair, running his hands through his hair. "I guess Jesus made it pretty clear to the old Pharisee, Nicodemus, didn't He?"

The Elder smiled as he leaned forward on the table, elbows planted on either side of his old Bible. "It was one of the few times that Jesus and a Pharisee had a normal conversation, wasn't it? And later in that same chapter, John the Baptist says much the same thing," and he looked to the text before him and read:

"Whoever believes in the Son has eternal life, but whoever rejects the Son will not see life, for God's wrath remains on him."[13]

"So, it's not just Matthew, or the other Synoptic Gospel writers," I said, adding a few more lines in my journal, painfully aware that my handwriting possessed none of the elegance (or legibility) of the Elder's.

"Even the Gospel written by John, the 'apostle of love', records Jesus' words about a separation; and that it all depends on how people respond to Him."

The Younger leaned so far back in his chair that I thought he would tip over, as he stared pensively at the artwork on the far wall. "That is *not* the answer I was hoping for, to be honest," he admitted finally, lowering all four legs of his chair back to the floor.

Retrieving his copy of the list I'd provided, he continued as he perused it. "But you can't avoid it. It's right there in black and white, in every Gospel. So no matter what I'd *hoped* the Kingdom would be like..." Plainly at a loss for words, his voice trailed off.

"Just like the people in the first century," I said suddenly, as the mental picture began to resolve itself into clarity. "The Kingdom is coming, but not in the way we'd expected, or would like to believe."

The Elder nodded, a fatherly expression on his lined face. "And the Kingdom has never been about us, has it? We don't simply add Jesus, and the rule and reign of His Kingdom, to our already-busy lives. We join what Jesus is already doing, and has been doing, long before we had any idea it was even happening. The Kingdom has been expanding for a very long time."

The Elder shifted gears abruptly, his chair scraping on the floor slightly as he changed position with a burst of renewed energy.

"And if I may borrow your phrase," he indicated the Younger, "Jesus *did* introduce an unexpected 'wrinkle': that the forgiveness of sins was somehow connected to the arrival of the Kingdom."

Donning his reading glasses once more, he read:

> "The saved remnant will be pardoned and forgiven, for their sins will be cast into the depths of the sea (Mic. 7:18-20). God will make a new covenant and will inscribe his law in the heart, granting a perfect fellowship with himself and the forgiveness of sins (Jer. 31:31-34, cf. also Ezek. 18:31; 36:22-28)."[14]

The Younger also sat up a little straighter in his chair, his posture unconsciously mimicking that of the Elder, as he industriously flipped digital pages in his e-reader. "I remember reading that same section, but I highlighted a different quote:

> "Jesus did not promise the forgiveness of sins; he bestowed it. He did not simply assure men of the future fellowship of the Kingdom; he invited men into fellowship with himself as the bearer of the Kingdom."[15]

"And when the disciples preached the 'gospel of the Kingdom' after Pentecost," I put in, making the connection even as the Younger had, "*that's* why they included 'forgiveness of sins' in the message. It wasn't just warning of the impending separation, it was also the offer of forgiveness of sins through Jesus the Messianic King."

The Elder suddenly clapped his hands together, startling both the Younger and I. "Ah yes, the Kingdom of God *is* coming, my friends, and to use a Biblical metaphor, the groomsmen will be overjoyed when the Groom arrives."[16]

He rubbed his hands together, looking around as if anticipating Jesus to walk through the door of the café at any moment. "Let's take a quick break, shall we, and then have a look at the parables Jesus used to describe the Kingdom. What do you say?"

"Sounds good to me," I agreed, stretching as I realized how long we'd been sitting in our wooden chairs. "How about another round of coffees? My treat."

The Younger twisted around in his chair to steal a look at the espresso bar, and turned back with a chuckle. "It looks like our cheerful Barista is still telling everyone about her lost-and-found ring. Believe it or not, I think she's even more hyper now than when we first came in. Are you sure you want to hear the story all over again?"

I had pulled out a twenty-dollar bill as he was speaking, but before I could answer, the Elder plucked it from my fingers as he rose stiffly from his chair.

"I'll go," he announced cheerfully. "There's something that just seems – well, *right* – hearing her story one more time. Especially today."

Before I could protest, he set off toward the espresso bar, excusing himself past other patrons in the narrow confines between the tables.

Enter Jesus Notes

1. *The Presence of the Future*, 230
2. George Eldon Ladd, *Crucial Questions about the Kingdom of God* (William B. Eerdmans Publishing Company, Grand Rapids, Mich., 1952), 64
3. Exodus 32:26
4. Joshua 24:15
5. 1 Kings 18:21
6. Matthew 3:7-10
7. Matthew 13:36-43
8. Matthew 13:47-50
9. Matthew 25:31-46
10. Mark 9:42-48; Mark 12:1-9 (specifically verse 9); Mark 13:26-27 (gathering 'elect' to Jesus implies that the 'non-elect' are not); Mark 16:15-16
11. *The Presence of the Future*, 226
12. John 3:16-18
13. John 3:36
14. *The Presence of the Future*, 213
15. Ibid., 217
16. Luke 5:33-35

Further Conversations

Do you have the three symbols in plain view of the group? (A subtle hint.)

1. Agree/Disagree: God is all-powerful and sovereign, but He doesn't always get what He wants.
2. Has God ever shown you something through another person, even if they – like the Barista in this chapter – do not see themselves as a 'person of faith'? What did God show you?
3. Look at the list of Bible verses where Jesus teaches/ expects that there will be a future separation of people when the Kingdom comes completely *(Appendix 1)*. Take turns in your group and read each of the verses out loud (yes, all of them.) What kind of reaction are you feeling after reading them all?
4. If Jesus spent so much time teaching about the coming separation, is it dishonest for us to ignore or hide it? At the same time, *how* we speak the truth is just as important as speaking the truth – how do we speak of this separation *and* be loving, respectful and inclusive of others?

Extra Credit:

1. You've already read all the verses in Appendix 1; you've done plenty. Have another round of coffee and enjoy conversations with your group.

chapter Eight
storyteller

It may be awhile before he returns, I mused, as the Elder made his way toward the front counter. *Even if the Barista doesn't share the entire saga of the ring again.*

The Younger, apparently arriving at the same conclusion, turned towards me as another thought occurred to him. "So, let me see if I've got this straight: When Jesus started preaching 'the Kingdom is near', the people got excited because it meant the Messiah had arrived, whom they believed would usher in the Kingdom rule and reign of God on earth. Except that Jesus, as the Messiah, didn't come in the way they expected. And Jesus surprised them by teaching that their inclusion in the Kingdom was entirely dependent on how they responded to Him. Or am I just repeating myself?"

Over the Younger's shoulder, I could see that the Elder had reached the front of the line, and was speaking with the glowing Barista again. "As our learned friend would say, repetition isn't a bad thing," I replied, looking back to the

Younger. “I think the main point we’ve emphasized this afternoon is that participation in the Kingdom *does* require a decision from us.”

The Younger looked at me for a long moment, then sighed as his gaze returned to the table in front of him. “Why is that such a hard concept these days? I mean, there are so many different opinions about what the Kingdom is or isn’t, who is in it or who isn’t, and how can anyone know...” His voice trailed off as he shook his head.

Then he straightened in his chair with a new note of resolve in his voice. “I can understand now why Ladd started us back in the Old Testament. In order to understand what the Kingdom meant in Jesus’ time, we had to dig into the background first. And to understand how the Kingdom applies to us *now*, we’ll need to dig into how Jesus explained the Kingdom when He came."

I pointed at my denim-covered journal, lying open on the table between us. “That’s why I'm looking forward to discussing the Parables. The stories Jesus told to describe the Kingdom are going to be very educational, not to mention challenging.”

The Younger’s body language betrayed his eagerness to dive into an exploration about the Kingdom in the Parables. “What I found significant,” he said with immediate enthusiasm, “was just how *many* of the parables were specifically about the Kingdom. Really, you could say that they’re *all* about the Kingdom, directly or indirectly. But it was fascinating to see how many of the parables were given explicitly to explain the Kingdom, and yet other parables seemed to deliberately cloud the issue."

We were so absorbed in our conversation that neither of us noticed the Elder making his way back to our table. Seemingly out of nowhere, he was suddenly here, carrying a plastic tray heavily burdened with far more than just a second round of coffee. I couldn't speak for the Younger, but the sight of the bagels on the tray made me realize just how hungry I was.

"Well, the two of you appear to be deep in thought," commented the Elder cheerily, motioning as if to set the heavy-laden tray on the table. The Younger and I quickly moved to clear enough space for it, and the Elder set his burden down with a relieved sigh. "What have you two been talking about, whilst I was sharing the joy of our barista a second time?"

Before either of us could reply, he continued thoughtfully, as he began removing items from the tray. "Did you know she's a fine arts student at the college down the road? Her dream in life is to someday become a professional photographer."

The Younger said nothing, and I wasn't about to admit that I couldn't even recall her name, despite frequenting the *Genesis* on a regular basis. It was a further embarrassment to realize that, like all the employees of the café, she wore a nametag. The Elder looked at each of us, appearing somewhat surprised by our silence, and I knew that he was sensing what he liked to call a 'teachable moment'.

As he shared out the bagels that he'd bought along with fresh coffee, the Elder quietly admonished, "How can we ever say 'the kingdom is near' to those around us, if we don't take the time to even know their names, or have any kind of relational connection with them?"

"Thanks, Pastor," cracked the Younger weakly, although judging by the look on his face, he felt as convicted as I did. "Just when I think I'm getting stuff sorted, you go and throw a monkey wrench of some kind into the mix."

The Elder laughed as he began to spread cream cheese – non-fat, no doubt – across his bagel. "Aren't you the one who is always concerned that there is a practical application to our beliefs? I would like to suggest that there is nothing more *practical* than getting to know the people around us. But getting back to my original question, what were the two of you discussing while I was gone?"

The Younger quickly filled him in, while I paged through my journal, reviewing the notes I'd made on Jesus' parables about the Kingdom.

"Well, you certainly didn't waste any time while I was away," observed the Elder, as the Younger finished his summary. "Which leads quite naturally, as you've already noticed, to Jesus' parables about the Kingdom, doesn't it?"

I realized that he'd been looking at my notes, so I summarized my own thoughts as concisely as possible. "First, Jesus claimed to be the Messiah who was bringing the Kingdom, and according to all four Gospels, our response to that claim is all-important. Second, there were several schools of thought about the Kingdom that had developed over the years, and these had a big impact on peoples' expectations. And finally, Jesus re-wrote a lot of these expectations by teaching us what *He* meant when He said 'the Kingdom is near'. And one of His primary methods of explaining the Kingdom was through the parables that He taught."

"In other, less long-winded words," the Younger interjected, rolling his eyes, "Jesus is setting the record straight about what the Kingdom really is, and how participation in it works."

The Elder set the plastic tray on floor, wedged upright between his chair and the wall for safekeeping. "I must confess: I have been looking forward to exploring the parables ever since we began to study the Kingdom. And, of course, to explore them together with two fine, upstanding young men such as yourselves," he finished, gifted as always at defusing the verbal sparring between the Younger and I.

Recognizing the hint that we should move on, I began buttering my own bagel. "Thanks, by the way, for going 'above and beyond' with this," I replied, indicating the food. "And fresh coffee is always appreciated, of course." The Younger made affirming sounds as he nodded, already enjoying his own share of the bagels.

"You are both most welcome," smiled the Elder, nodding mischievously in my direction. "It was *your* money I was happily spending, after all."

"So, tell me," he continued, taking a bite of his bagel, "what main ideas in the parables have you discovered? Aside from several of the parables being found in more than one Gospel, I mean. Did you find any recurring themes among them?"

The Younger pulled out his e-reader as he swallowed the last mouthful of his bagel, switching to the Bible program he'd opened earlier.

"Well, I know we've talked about the 'separation dynamic' already, but I notice that there are several parables dealing with the wheat being separated from the chaff, and the good fish/bad fish" – he paused momentarily, before adding mischievously, "green fish/blue fish?"

"The sheep and the goats come to mind," I added, pretending – as was the Elder – that I hadn't heard the Younger's Dr. Seuss-inspired comment. "But I think I'd like to leave that specific parable until later, when we're looking at the ethics of the Kingdom. There are plenty of other parables, like the ones you just mentioned, that show the coming separation."

Referring to my notes, I pointed out, "Some of the parables also make specific mention that the coming separation would be a result of deliberately refusing God's invitation. For example, there are two versions of the story of the Banquet, one in Matthew[1], and the other in Luke[2]. The recurring theme is that those who were originally invited to God's banquet, the Kingdom, refused to come. And so the invitation to the banquet was given to others, who *did* respond. And I note that the audience for these parables was the religious leaders."

The Elder nodded in agreement. "And Jesus told the parable of the tenants in Matthew's gospel[3], Luke's[4], and," – his eyes twinkled as he looked at me – "in *Mark*[5], to also describe the religious leaders even more pointedly than the parable of the banquet. So pointedly, in fact, that they decided to murder Jesus after they heard it."

"Wow," exclaimed the Younger incredulously, wiping crumbs from his fingers. "Talk about being 'all hard to teach'! Even when they knew Jesus was speaking directly to them, they still refused to change their minds. It doesn't matter how many times I read that, it always amazes me how hard-headed they were."

"Yeah, it's mind-boggling," I agreed, finishing my bagel and stacking my plate on top of the Younger's, as we attempted to create some space on the crowded tabletop. "But when we group these parables together, I'm not satisfied that they actually tell us much *about* the Kingdom. I mean, it confirms Ladd's statement about the Kingdom requiring a response, and the religious leaders chose wrong. But it's still not a good description of the Kingdom itself."

The Younger flipped digitally to his own notes as he began his answer to my statement. "What struck me was how *subversive* the Kingdom was in the parables. I mean, some of parables teach that the Kingdom is arriving 'secretly', under the radar. The parable of the mustard seed, for instance, which is in three of the Gospels[6]. Jesus compares it to one of the smallest seeds, but said it would grow into a strong tree eventually. He doesn't explain *how* that happens, only that it does."

"And twice, in Matthew[7] and Luke[8], the mustard seed parable shows up with the parable of yeast." Once again, the Younger began to enumerate each of his points on his fingertips. "One, it's small; two, you can't see it working but it is, and three, eventually, it affects everything."

The Younger flipped another digital page as he continued, "And last but not least, there's the parable of the seed that grows in secret, in Mark's gospel[9]. They all paint an image of a *subversive* Kingdom, as opposed to the 'big bang' of the Day of the Lord. That must have driven the apocalyptists crazy."

The Elder folded his hands, resembling a professor about to deliver a lecture more than ever. *Why did he choose to become an English teacher instead of a seminary professor,* I wondered to myself, not for the first time.

"The hidden nature of the Kingdom is something that many people have wrestled to understand over the centuries," he began slowly, studying his own hands as he spoke. "I think that our 'key to interpretation' might be found in one of Jesus' most well-known stories: the Parable of the Sower. Although if you look at it carefully, this parable is more about the *seed*, than about the sower."

Raising his eyes, his gaze favored each of us in turn as he continued. "It's also repeated in all three of the Synoptic gospels: Matthew[10], Mark[11] and Luke[12], which I believe suggests that we pay careful attention to it."

Pages rustled as the Elder and I turned to our analog Bibles, while the Younger soundlessly perused his digital copy. At the Elder's suggestion, each of us looked up the parable of the Sower and the Seed in a different Gospel.

For a few moments, the only discernible exception to the ambient sounds of the café was the scratching of my pen, as I scribbled some hasty notes.

The Elder broke the silence first, waiting with characteristic patience until the Younger and I had finished our quick re-reading. "I would like to suggest that there are several themes to be found within this parable."

And just as the Younger would have done, he began to tick off each point on his fingers. *I wonder which one of them influenced the other in that habit,* was the thought that crossed my mind as he began.

"First of all, the sower is only incidental to the parable. The *real* subject of the parable is the seed, which Jesus tells us is the message of the Kingdom. Second, the seed doesn't have the same effect everywhere it goes. Simply sowing the seed doesn't produce an automatic, one-size-fits-all result." He paused for a moment, allowing the point to settle into our thinking.

"Third," he continued, after a quick sip of his coffee, "we find the 'kingdoms in conflict' dynamic at work again. The devil, also called the evil one or Satan, depending on which Gospel you're reading, comes and steals away the message from the hard-hearted. Or from the hard-headed, if you prefer."

"Fourth, the message of the Kingdom appears to have *short-term results* in some cases. Eventually, of course, either persecution or an obsession with the cares of this life will kill it off. And finally," the Elder switched hands for his last point, "there is the response of the 'good soil', which brings a harvest. The metaphors in this parable are quite reminiscent of John the Baptist's words at the beginning of Matthew: the necessity of producing the 'fruit of repentance'."

The Elder removed his reading glasses, gesturing with both hands as he continued. "And most intriguing of all, this parable, and the explanation Jesus gives of it, is deliberately subversive, if I may borrow your term." That last comment was directed to the Younger, who nodded absently as he continued to scan the parable before him. "The parable wasn't immediately understood by everyone who heard it. Yet even here, the message of the Kingdom required a response: which 'soil' will you be? Hard, rocky, thorny, or good?"

"For those who have ears to hear," the Younger said quietly, pensively.

The Elder pulled his copy of Ladd out from under his large Bible. "Ladd's thoughts on this parable connect as well with the other parables you brought up: the mustard seed, the yeast, and the seed growing secretly:

> "The Kingdom is working quietly, secretly among men. It does not force itself upon them; it must be willingly received... There is no emphasis on the harvest, either in the parable or in its

interpretation. The single emphasis is upon the nature of the sowing - the present action of God's Kingdom."[13]

The Younger sat back in his chair, placing his reader back on the table with a sigh. "Okay, on one hand, I understand that Jesus wants people to *actively choose* the Kingdom, instead of some kind of passive acceptance. But the implications of *not* choosing the Kingdom are so serious, I can't get my head around why He wouldn't make it clearer, and easier, for people to become part of the Kingdom of God."

There was a moment of silence around the table. I could see that the Elder knew what he wanted to say in response to the Younger's implied question, but out of his deep respect for others, he wasn't about to jump right in.

It was just one more example of the Elder's maturity, which I hoped someday to emulate.

"If the Kingdom is the 'rule and reign' of Jesus, how could there be some sort of 'auto-kingdom' response?" the Elder asked quietly, delicately.

"Submitting to the rule and reign of God is a conscious decision," he continued. "It is all about allegiance to the King, which is not something that comes automatically. There is quite a difference between the authority a king has over his realm – his power – and his subjects choosing *loyalty* to him – a relationship."

The Younger nodded without speaking, pondering the implications of the Elder's words.

"That's quite different from how we usually understand a king's authority over the subjects of his kingdom," I observed carefully, hoping I hadn't created a rabbit trail away from the point the Elder wanted to drive home. "In the first century, I doubt anyone felt any sense of *relationship* with King Herod. Their loyalty or lack of loyalty was politically motivated, not relational. By introducing a relationship to His Kingdom authority, Jesus was re-writing their expectations again."

The Younger snapped his fingers as another thought occurred to him. "Jesus' lament over Jerusalem[14]," he exclaimed, an expression of dawning comprehension spreading across his face. "He came as their King, but His own subjects refused Him[15]. But the way he addresses Jerusalem for rejecting Him sounds more like a heart-broken parent than a political leader."

The Elder replaced his reading glasses on his nose in a quick gesture, obviously eager to go deeper in our conversation. "Ah, it would appear your insights have given me an opportune moment to point out another significant aspect of the Kingdom. One that Jesus' listeners could hardly have been expecting." He pulled his copy of Ladd closer, flipping the pages quickly to a section that was almost entirely highlighted in yellow. Pausing as he adjusted his reading glasses, he added apologetically, "This is a somewhat lengthier passage. Please bear with me."

> "God is seeking out sinners and inviting them to submit themselves to his reign that he might be their Father. An inseparable relationship exists

> between the Kingdom of God and his Fatherhood; and it is particularly notable that this affinity between the two concepts appears most frequently in an eschatological setting. In the eschatological salvation, the righteous will enter into the Kingdom of their Father (Matthew 13:43).
>
> "It is the Father who has prepared for the blessed this eschatological inheritance of the Kingdom (Matthew 15:34). It is the Father who will bestow upon Jesus' disciples the gift of the Kingdom (Luke 12:32). The highest gift of God's Fatherhood is participation in God's sovereignty which is to be exercised over all the world.
>
> "In that day, Jesus will enjoy a renewed fellowship with his disciples in the Father's Kingdom (Matthew 26:29). Since the greatest joy as children of God is that of sharing the blessings of the Kingdom, Jesus taught his disciples to pray, "Our Father who are in heaven... thy kingdom come" (Matthew 6:9-10). Clearly Kingship and Fatherhood are closely related concepts."[16]

The Elder removed his reading glasses once more, sweeping aside a few remaining crumbs as he carefully set them down. "God as Father was not a completely new concept to the Israelites in Jesus' day, of course. But Jesus went out of His way to emphasize that God is both King *and* Father. We must hold these two ideas in dynamic tension. Stray to one extreme, and we paint God as sovereign, but distant and unapproachable. If we go too much to the other extreme, we will end up with a picture of a lovingly irresponsible buddy-in-the-sky who comes at our beck and call."

Leaning forward, his voice remaining at the same volume but with increasing intensity, the Elder expounded, "God is our sovereign King, with all that that implies. And God is also our Father, with all the relational implications that come with that. Whenever we emphasize one aspect at the expense of the other, we will reap an incomplete understanding of who God really is."

Another moment of thoughtful silence followed the Elder's impassioned words, as each of us meditated on God as both sovereign King and heavenly Father.

The Younger was the first to break the reverie of the moment. "I remember being at a weekend conference during college, and the speaker's topic was 'the Father-heart of God'," he mused, recalling the event. "His thesis statement was Jesus' words to Phillip: 'anyone who has seen Me, has seen the Father'.[17] And for the rest of the weekend, we went through the entire Gospel of John, since that's the gospel where Phillip's words are written down. We looked at each and every story of how Jesus interacted with people, and how that revealed something of the Father's character."

"A tour of the *Gospel According to St. John* is always a good thing," smiled the Elder, shifting his copy of Ladd back underneath his large, leather-bound Bible. "And I strongly believe that it's significant when Jesus connects the in-breaking rule and reign of the Kingdom of God with an emphasis on God as 'Father'. And at the risk of repeating myself, which we older folk are known to do from time to time, we need to hold firmly," and he clenched both hands as if tightening his grip on something tangible, "that God is both King *and* Father."

The Younger straightened suddenly in his chair, pantomiming a slap to his own forehead. "And when His disciples asked to be taught how to pray, Jesus told them to pray to 'our Father'[18], not 'our King'. I've known that since, well, *forever*, but I never realized the significance of it until now."

The pages of the Elder's Bible made a whispery sound as he flipped with practiced ease to the Gospel of Luke.

"Perhaps it would be fitting at this juncture to look at one of the most well-known of Jesus' parables (next to the Good Samaritan, that is): the Parable of the Prodigal Son[19]." With practiced ease, the Elder retrieved his reading glasses, and deftly slid them into place on the bridge of his nose, one-handed.

"Or the Parable of the Lost Son," I threw in, as I looked up the same passage in my own Bible. "At least, that's the subtitle that I have in my version."

The Younger leaned back with an air of smug superiority. You would have to know him well to recognize when he was play-acting; that's how convincing he could be at times. "I can read it to you in *any number* of Bible versions. What's your preference today?" he offered loftily, holding his e-reader as if it had been hand-delivered by the archangel Gabriel himself.

The Elder simply looked at him, peering over his reading glasses with a patient but bemused look. "Are you quite done?" he asked with mock severity, turning his attention back to his Bible.

"This parable could also be called the Parable of the Waiting Father, as other theologians have suggested," he continued with barely a pause. "It's actually a study in contrasts between God's heart for the prodigal son, compared to the older brother's attitude. And in context, I believe the identity of the 'older brother' was abundantly clear: the Pharisees, who were offended by the kind of company Jesus was willing to share table fellowship with."

"And the kind of people Jesus was accepting into His Father's kingdom," interjected the Younger, immediately making the connection.

"It's also another example of the Old Testament concept of the *God who comes*", continued the Elder, nodding in agreement with the Younger's words. "Except that in Jesus' time, God was coming and seeking people for relationship in His Kingdom, even those whom the Pharisees deemed unworthy of the Kingdom."

The Elder pulled his copy of *Jesus and the Kingdom* from underneath his Bible again, gently smoothing its pages as he began to read.

> "The central truth of all three parables is that of the yearning God. God is like one who seeks for the lost sheep, who searches for the lost coin, who longs for the return of the

prodigal. This is a parable about the Father, not about the son."[20]

The Elder removed his reading glasses again, gesturing with them as he became more animated. "The *God who comes* is the same one who would leave the ninety-nine sheep behind, in order to search for one that is missing. The Kingdom requires a response from us, that much is certainly clear.

"However, God is not passively biding His time on a cloud somewhere. He is actively searching for those who are lost – those who are outside the Kingdom. For example, notice how Jesus concludes and applies the parable of the lost sheep:

"I tell you that in the same way, there will be *more* joy in heaven over one sinner who repents than over ninety-nine righteous persons who need no repentance."[21]

The Elder folded his glasses and returned them to his pocket, leaning forward to emphasize his next words. "In the Kingdom, God is both King and Father. But more than this, He is the *seeking* Father. Jesus is, Himself, a 'living parable': the Son of God who has come to seek, and in so doing, revealing to us *who* may enter His Kingdom."

"And it's not who the holier-than-thou Pharisees would have expected," commented the Younger dryly.

"Or who we would expect today," I added, mindful of our tendency to assume we were incapable of repeating the errors of the Pharisees. "It all boils down to receiving God's gift."

The Elder uttered a wordless exclamation, frowning with consternation at his wristwatch. “I deeply apologize for leaving so abruptly,” he said urgently, “but our presence is required elsewhere in less than twenty minutes.”

“It's Tuesday?” blurted the Younger in consternation. “You’re right; we’re serving dinner at the homeless shelter!” He leaped to his feet, nearing knocking the stacked plates off the edge of the table as he hastily pulled his jacket on.

After witnessing the near-disaster of the Younger’s hasty exit, the Elder and I were more cautious as we got up from the table, our chairs scraping on the floor. As the Elder carefully replaced his books into his ancient leather satchel, I handed the e-reader to the Younger and picked up my Bible and journal.

As the three of us began to wind our way through the crowded gauntlet of tables, we spied the exuberant Barista, once more regaling her newest audience at the espresso bar with the saga of the ring. “Far be it from me to hold you guys up,” I said as we neared the door, “but I wanted to say thanks for today. We covered even more ground that I thought we would.”

“Yeah, I guess we did,” agreed the Younger, pausing with his hand on the doorknob. Looking to the Elder, he commented, “My only regret is that we didn’t have time for the Parable of the Lost Coin. It’s such a great metaphor: the desperation of the search, the moment of discovery, and the ‘evangelism’, if you will, of telling the story to your neighbors. It's too bad we didn't have the time to explore that parable as well."

The Elder favored us both with a strange look. "Didn't we?" he asked lightly, the tone of his voice betraying the unspoken suggestion that somehow, somewhere, we had missed something. The Younger looked quizzically from the Elder to me, eyebrows raised, as perplexed as I was.

The Elder half-turned to glance briefly but pointedly at the exuberant Barista, who was no less enthusiastic in telling her tale now than when we had first arrived. "For those who have ears to hear," he murmured softly with a shake of his head, as he pushed open the door and stepped briskly into the falling dusk.

Storyteller Notes

1. Matthew 22:1-14
2. Luke 14:15-24
3. Matthew 21:33-46
4. Luke 20:9-19
5. Mark 12:1-12
6. Matthew 13:31-32; Mark 4:30-32; Luke 13:18-19
7. Matthew 13:33
8. Luke 13:20-21
9. Mark 4:26-29
10. Matthew 13:1-23
11. Mark 4:1-20
12. Luke 8:4-15
13. *The Presence of the Future*, 230
14. Matthew 23:37-39; Luke 13:34-35
15. John 1:10-11
16. *The Presence of the Future*, 178-179 (italics in original)
17. John 14:6-10
18. Matthew 6:5-15; Luke 11:1-13
19. Luke 15:11-32
20. *The Presence of the Future*, 182
21. Luke 15:7

Further Conversations

1. Divide into two groups. One group will brainstorm a list entitled "King" and the other group will brainstorm a list entitled "Father". Each group will brainstorm as many implications of viewing God according to their list as possible. Compare lists and see how much of a fuller view of God results.
2. On the other hand, what kind of implications could result if we only held a one-sided view of God, either only as King or only as Father?
3. Read the parables of the Lost Sheep, the Lost Coin, and the Prodigal Son – all found (coincidentally?) in the same chapter: Luke 15. What is Jesus' conclusion to each of these three parables?
4. Who are the people in today's society that would be considered "undesirables" in the Kingdom? People with addictions? Racists? Child molester? Men with a history of violence towards women? What does "grace" look like for these people?

<u>Extra Credit:</u>

Jesus told Philip: "Anyone who has seen me has seen the Father." (John 14:9)

1. Read through the Gospel According to St. John and take note of each time Jesus speaks to or in some way interacts with another person(s). How would you describe Jesus' character in each instance, and therefore, the character of His Father?

chapter Nine
kitchen justice

The chiming of the doorbell, an unexpected intrusion into an otherwise tranquil Saturday morning, startled the Elder in the midst of his self-appointed weekend project.

Glancing quickly down at his attire, he was relieved to discover that he would suffer no personal embarrassment by answering the bell.

Deftly navigating the various piles he'd created in the bedroom, he made his way towards the front door.

The Elder recognized his guest as he entered the kitchen, looking down the short hallway beyond to the front door. Three rectangular panes of glass, set in a diagonal pattern in the upper third of the sturdy wooden door, allowed natural light into his home, while also revealing the identity of any visitor.

"Good morning!" exclaimed the Younger cheerfully, stuffing his car keys with one hand into the pocket of his denim jacket, a comfortable but uncharacteristically casual choice of clothing for him. Two cups of coffee steamed an enticing greeting from a cardboard tray carefully balanced in his other hand.

The Elder smiled in greeting as he held the screen door at bay, allowing the Younger to enter his modest two-bedroom bungalow. "I wasn't expecting you for another hour or so," he offered by way of explanation, as the Younger eased past him. "But when you arrive bearing the sweet nectar of the coffee bean, an open door and a warm welcome will always be yours."

"I know I'm a little early," the Younger admitted, transferring the coffee tray to the Elder as he shrugged out of his jacket, "but I thought bringing coffee would be a suitable bribe. Or maybe penance. I didn't interrupt anything important, did I?"

The Elder opened his mouth as if to answer, but paused for the briefest of moments. The Younger's attention was distracted by hanging his denim jacket on one of the available coat hooks, and he didn't see the Elder's gaze wander to the slightly-faded photographs that hung in frames just inside the entrance-way. Nodding his head slightly, as if he'd come to a decision of sorts, he finally answered, as the Younger turned toward him again, e-reader retrieved from an inner pocket of his jacket.

"To be perfectly honest, I was navigating one of those difficult thresholds in the grieving process," he stated quietly and matter-of-factly. There was a recognizably far-off look in his eye as his gaze lingered on the faded black and white photograph of a smiling young couple on their wedding day. "It's one of those markers in the journey: the day you finally pack up and part with your wife's belongings from the bedroom closet."

Only a friendship as well established as theirs could salvage the moment from a debilitating awkwardness. Although in truth, the Younger found himself in one of those rare instances where he could think of nothing to say, as he looked sadly and with sympathy at his friend.

The Elder took a deep breath, rousing himself from the emotion of the moment, smiling again as he handed over the coffee tray. "I realize it's been three years, but I've learned that I'm in good company: many people struggle to part with their spouse's personal effects until much later. And when the time finally comes, well, you just buckle down and *do it*, but the moment is not without its own unique and poignant nostalgia."

The Younger nodded wordlessly, determined to *not* say anything well intentioned but ultimately trite. He followed the Elder into the cozy kitchen, still carrying the coffees, as he glanced around the meticulously organized room. *A place for everything, and everything in its place,* the Younger thought to himself with wry amusement.

The Elder took the coffees from him, freeing them from the confines of the tray and setting them down on the checkered tablecloth covering the kitchen table. The Elder's copy of *Jesus and the Kingdom*, as well as his battered old Bible, already occupied a significant part of the table's surface.

"Oh, good Lord and butter," the Elder sighed with feigned consternation, as he removed the plastic lids from the cups. "You've *poisoned* it." The Younger looked from his cup to the Elder's, noticing immediately with consternation that despite his scrupulously clear instructions in the drive-through, *both* of the coffees clearly had had cream added to them.

"I don't believe it," the Younger muttered, more disappointed than the Elder appeared to be. "I *told* them: one black, and one double-double."

"I wouldn't worry about it," smiled the Elder, taking a sip. "While I prefer coffee to be black – the way God drinks it – I'm not *completely* inflexible in my old age." Noting that the Younger barely smiled in response, he set his cup down and laid his hand on the Younger's arm. "Let me tell you something about the grieving process, my friend: it's not some monolithic dark cloud that colors my every waking moment, forever and ever, amen."

"Certainly, at the beginning, the grief can be devastating," he conceded. "But as time goes on, you learn how to embrace the process, and its ability to overwhelm and paralyze you becomes less and less. So, please, don't feel uncomfortable that you arrived when you did."

The Elder's eyes crinkled as a warm smile spread across his face, "And please, I beg you, don't be shocked that I can move from nostalgic sadness as I look at a framed memory, to making my traditionally feeble joke about coffee only moments later. Believe it or not, one does not become one-dimensional, emotionally speaking, during the season of grieving."

The Younger relaxed, at least somewhat, still not completely sure how appropriate it would be to return to their usual banter. "To be honest, it *did* seem a little strange that you would prep for our morning discussion on Kingdom ethics by cleaning out your wife's closet."

The Elder took another sip of his coffee. "I hadn't thought of it as *preparing*," he admitted, acknowledging the apparent incongruence with a small shrug. "It was simply one of those 'life must go on' moments. And I promise you: I will *thoroughly* enjoy our conversation, even with poisoned coffee. And later, when I return to my task, I will also fully embrace the emotions of *that* moment."

Without further ado, the Elder turned to rummage through a kitchen cabinet, just to the left of the single sink. The Younger shook his head in admiration, as he retrieved the e-reader from his messenger bag.

"I learn so much from you," he murmured under his breath, just as the Elder, with a pleased exclamation, located the object he was searching for. Returning to the table with a flourish, the Elder triumphantly placed a ceramic saltshaker, shaped and painted to resemble a hamburger, on the table between them.

"Just a reminder," he explained, gesturing towards the saltshaker, "that the ethical teachings of Jesus had a great deal in common with the Old Testament prophets and their concern for the ethical behavior of the Israelites. Jesus' teachings established the standard for ethics in the Kingdom. There was no dichotomy between submitting to the rule and reign of His Father, and abiding by the ethical teachings of Jesus."

The Younger nodded as he arranged the various documents in his e-reader. "I've been really looking forward to this discussion," he began, "because as you know, I'm always looking for the practical application of the faith. And there's nothing more practical than the Sermon on the Mount. Is there anything you want to highlight first? Or can I steer us into the Sermon on the Mount right away?"

The Elder smiled mischievously, as he reached over to retrieve his copy of *Jesus and the Kingdom*, as well as his large Bible. "My first observation is that you use the phrase 'practical application' almost as often as I refer to black coffee as 'the way God drinks it'."

The Younger's coffee cup froze in mid-air as he, mouth agape, recognized the truth in the Elder's statement. Chuckling, the Elder continued. "But in all seriousness, two things come to mind, although they are very closely connected to each other.

"First, I would want to keep in mind that this is the Kingdom of the *Father*. There is a familial relationship which everyone in the Kingdom enjoys with God. It's absolutely *fascinating* to read the entire Sermon on the Mount, chapters five through seven in Matthew's Gospel, and take note of just how many times Jesus uses the word *Father*. And second, I would like to suggest that we not put the theological cart before the horse."

Anticipating the question behind the inquisitive expression that came over the Younger's face, he continued without missing a beat, turning to the passage he'd previously book-marked for just this occasion. "What I mean by that is perhaps best explained in light of Ladd's own words:

> "A righteousness exceeding that of the scribes and the Pharisees was demanded for entrance into the eschatological Kingdom (Matthew 5:20). This righteousness includes freedom from anger, from lust, from retaliation (Matthew 5:21-48). If the attainment of such perfect righteousness is left to human effort, no one can acquire it; it must be God's gift."[1]

> "Here is the very heart of Jesus' ethical teaching: the renunciation of self-attained righteousness and the willingness to become like children who have nothing and must receive everything."[2]

Looking up from his reading, the Elder nudged his reading glasses a little further down on his nose, so that his eyes met the Younger's over their rims.

"If we look at the Sermon on the Mount through the lens of what we must *do* in order to gain access into His Kingdom, we will completely miss the point. The ethical teachings of Jesus are the cart, not the horse."

The Younger listened intently, drawn by the quiet passion in the Elder's voice as he continued, "You see, Jesus did not intend that only our *faith* be simple and childlike, trusting in the goodness of the Father. He meant that we cannot 'earn' our way into the Kingdom by our good behavior. Part of being 'like a child' simply means that we must surrender our attempts at bettering ourselves, and merely – *receive."*

The Younger leaned back from the table, as he glanced down at the Sermon on the Mount on his e-reader. "That's actually quite a relief," he remarked thoughtfully, "because the ethical teachings of Jesus are even more intense than the Law in the Old Testament. For example, Jesus takes something like 'thou shalt not murder', which most people could honestly say 'never done it, check mark number one for me', and drives it even deeper. Now, if you're holding on to anger, you're just as guilty as if you pulled the trigger. Not to mention how He talked about adultery and lust, or loving enemies. If good ethical behavior was a pre-requisite to entering the Kingdom..." His voice trailed off and he heaved a heavy sigh.

The Elder smiled as he gestured with his hands. "Without exaggeration, you could say that Jesus is making it abundantly clear, even to the most self-righteous person in His audience: *you simply can't do it.* Apart from receiving the Kingdom as a gift, like a child, it's quite literally impossible."

The Younger folded his arms and leaned on the table once more, thinking through the implications. "Would you say this is related to what John the Baptist said at the beginning of Matthew, about 'producing fruit in keeping with righteousness'?[3] That if you receive the Kingdom 'like a child', then these are the kind of ethical changes that the Kingdom produces in you?"

The Elder adjusted his glasses back into reading position as he answered. "The true progression is simply: Kingdom first, ethics to follow. Of course, there will always be the human responsibility to co-operate. It's a fine line, in some ways; you don't earn the Kingdom, but rather you *reflect* the Kingdom. Or to be more precise, you reflect the *character* of the King."

The Elder turned again to his copy of Ladd, as he read with great enthusiasm and dramatic flair:

> "The setting of the Sermon on the Mount is this evil age (Matthew 5:13-16) where Jesus' followers are to display the character of their heavenly Father."[4]

Pausing for a moment, the Elder parenthetically added an editorial comment to Ladd. "This already-and-not-yet dynamic is an important one to keep in mind in numerous different ways, including our ethical behavior." His gaze returned to the pages before him as he resumed his reading.

> "Even as the Kingdom has invaded the evil age to bring to men in advance a partial but real experience of the blessings of the eschatological Kingdom, so is the righteousness of the Kingdom attainable, in part if not in perfection, in the

present order. Ethics, like the kingdom itself, stand in the tension between present realization and future eschatological perfection."[5]

The Elder glanced back up, a smile toying at the corners of his mouth. "I realize that I have a tendency to repeat myself at times, so you may recall my mentioning of Hebrews 10:14 before: 'by one sacrifice He has made perfect forever those who are being made holy'.

"It's a beautiful portrait of the already and the not-yet of the Kingdom. The Father views us in the *already* – 'made perfect forever' – even as we live daily in the *not-yet* – 'being made holy'. It's a liberating and inspiring revelation, wouldn't you say?"

The Younger exhaled a long, slow breath. "It's a *relief*, to be honest. It's not about pushing myself to 'earn' God's favor, or to prove that I am worthy of Him. Or even trying to repay Him somehow."

"And inspiring," finished the Elder, "because it confirms that we have the grace available to us, as the Holy Spirit guides and equips us, to actually bring forth the fruit of repentance.

"Which takes us full circle, back to some of Jesus' ethical teachings: the Parable of the Talents[6], and the Sheep and the Goats[7]."

The Younger frowned as he looked at his own notes. "I think I can see where you're going with this, but could I request that we include the Good Samaritan[8], and the Unmerciful Servant[9], while we're at it?"

"Certainly," concurred the Elder, folding his hands in front of him, "and feel free to go first, if you'd like."

The Younger laughed a little self-consciously, aware of his tendency to be impulsive and at times (truth be told), impatient in his restless energy. "Okay, I'll dive in first: next to the Prodigal Son, the Good Samaritan is probably the most well-known parable that Jesus told. If we are looking at it as a parable about ethics in the Kingdom, then a few questions stand out to me: who did the will of the Father, who *didn't*, and what are the implications?"

The Younger edged forward in his seat, picking up the saltshaker and squinting across it towards the Elder, as if he was sighting down the barrel of a rifle. "Jesus very bluntly informed the Pharisees that the prostitutes and 'sinners' were entering the Kingdom, while they were refusing it[10]. And, just in case they missed it, Jesus takes it to another level by comparing the Pharisees to a son who tells his father that he'll obey him, but doesn't. Their actions showed their true allegiance."

The Elder nodded, hands still folded and resting on his Bible. "And the connection to the *Good Samaritan* would be...?" he prompted us with a tilt of his head, eyebrows raised questioningly.

"The teacher of the law asked about inheriting 'eternal life', which Ladd says is really synonymous with the Kingdom[11]," replied the Younger, setting the saltshaker down on the table. "And the point of the Good Samaritan parable is that it was the *last* person you would expect – the Samaritan – who actually *did* the right thing, while the priest and the Levite, who *should* have known better, did nothing. Their actions revealed their true allegiance."

The Elder nodded, seeing the direction the Younger was going. "And in the parable of the Unmerciful Servant, we read of a servant who owed a debt so large that there was no way he could ever repay it. The king showed mercy and forgave the debt, and yet the servant was unwilling to forgive another servant for an extremely tiny debt. In the end, the first servant is called back before the king, who is furious that the servant could be forgiven so much, and yet be unwilling to forgive others for so little. How would you connect this parable to your thesis?"

The Younger switched applications in his e-reader, turning to Ladd's *The Presence of the Future*, as he answered. "The Parable of the Unmerciful Servant has a very similar application: that our actions reveal where our allegiance really is." Finding the page he was looking for, the Younger held up his e-reader as he read aloud.

> "The point of this parable is that when a man claims to have received the unconditioned and unmerited forgiveness of God, which is one of the gifts of the Kingdom, and then is unwilling to forgive relatively trivial offenses against himself, he denies the reality of his very profession of divine forgiveness and by his conduct contradicts the life and character of the Kingdom."[12]

The Younger lowered his e-reader to the checkered tablecloth once more, as he tried to summarize his line of thinking. "It keeps going back to John the Baptist's words about fruit, over and over again. The people who are entering the Kingdom, according to Jesus, are the ones who are showing its fruit. They are the ones actually *doing* what the Kingdom is about, not just giving passive lip service."

The Elder chuckled as he recognized, for the umpteenth time, the Younger's dogged insistence for theology to be grounded in practical, daily living. It was one of the characteristics he most appreciated and admired about his younger friend.

"You'll get no argument from me," the Elder replied light-heartedly, "especially in view of Jesus saying that only those who did the will of His Father would actually inherit the Kingdom.[13] There is definitely a sense of *active participation* in the Kingdom that is expected, even if we originally receive the Kingdom as children receiving a gift on Christmas Day."

The Elder paused briefly, frowning for a moment, as he framed his next question carefully. "Help me understand: I'm not sure I'm following your logic for including the Parable of the Unmerciful Servant in the same breath. It *does* fit into the category of Kingdom ethics – after all, Jesus made the same point when He instructed His disciples in what we now call the 'Lord's Prayer': if you don't forgive as the Father has forgiven you, then you negate the Father's forgiveness in your own life[14]. But I'm curious: why would you pair it with the Good Samaritan?"

The Younger chewed on his bottom lip for a second, a childhood habit he would have sworn had been broken years earlier. "Maybe I'm trying too hard to make it fit," he admitted with a sheepish expression, "or is my pragmatism affecting my theology?"

The Elder laughed but encouraged him to finish his thought before commenting.

The Younger leaned forward on his elbows, causing a slight squeak of complaint from his chair, speaking slowly as he talked himself through his own emerging thoughts. As was his habit, he began ticking off each point sequentially on his fingers.

"Well, my first thought was this: the point of the Good Samaritan is about who is actually *doing* the works of the Kingdom. My second thought was that in the Sermon on the Mount, Jesus regularly moved from the external – thou shall not commit murder – to the heart attitude, such as anger or lust."

The Younger paused for a moment as he tried to find the right words, before concluding, "And three, I guess I see the Unmerciful Servant parable doing the same thing: moving from the external to the heart attitude. The Samaritan was about our actions towards others, but the Unmerciful Servant is about our heart attitude. And my conclusion would be," he paused for just a moment, "that you have to combine the heart attitude *and* the practical actions. You can't depend on either one by itself."

The Elder made a gesture of tipping a non-existent hat in deference to the Younger's insightful comment. "You've hit that elusive balance that many of us have struggled to maintain. Saint James would be proud of you, for saying that we prove our faith to be genuine by our works."[15]

The Younger leaned back with a relieved sigh. "Were you just messing with my head? I was worried that you thought I was inventing some new heresy."

The Elder pulled his Bible back to the top of the pile on his side of the table, chuckling. "There aren't a lot of 'new' heresies, really, just old ones with a fresh marketing campaign. But no, I wasn't attempting to trip you up, if that's what you thought. I was honestly curious about how you were connecting the dots." Opening his Bible, he continued with barely a pause, "You will be pleased to hear that the parables I mentioned earlier also have a *very* strong emphasis on faith and practical works."

Sitting a little straighter in his chair, exuding a renewed air of eager anticipation, he adjusted his reading glasses once more. "First, the quick background: in the twenty-third chapter of Matthew, Jesus delivers His list of 'woes' on the Pharisees. Two things are significant for our discussion this morning: one, that Jesus is quite livid with the Pharisees and this is a pretty thorough denunciation, and two..." the Elder paused for emphasis before continuing, "the accusation against the Pharisees is that they claimed to be right with God, and yet they *didn't* 'bring forth fruit'. Jesus had a word for that: *hypocrite*."[16]

The Younger sighed. "That's a good description, no doubt about that," he observed dryly, "and people have been accusing Christians of the same ever since."

The Elder nodded in agreement, as he flipped through the pages of his Bible. "If the shoe fits... Such is the 'fruit' of *not* practicing what you preach."

Tapping the page before him, he went on. "Matthew has arranged this part of his gospel to contrast the hypocrisy of the Pharisees with what life in the Kingdom *should* look like. And the remainder of the chapter is filled with allusions to the eschatological Kingdom, which would come in the future."

Upon hearing the word *eschatological*, the Younger's eyes strayed to the collection of cooking utensils hanging above the gas stove behind the Elder, immediately picking out the unmistakable sight of the meat cleaver which had been the unintentional source of so much drama.

The Elder followed his gaze, twisting in his chair. Spotting the infamous utensil, he rose from his chair with a conspiratorial grin, retrieving the cleaver and placing it next to the hamburger-shaped saltshaker. "Ah, the memories of our misspent youth. Now, where was I? Oh yes, in the following chapter, Matthew twenty-four, Jesus is warning the disciples that the hour of the future Kingdom's arrival is unknown, even to Him. So, the disciples are warned to be watchful *and* to keep *doing*. That's the background to these final three parables in Matthew."

The Elder paused once more, adjusting his glasses as he scanned the pages before him. "I would like to suggest that the order of these parables moves from the lesser impact, to the greater. For example, the Parable of the Ten Virgins[17] is a story that illustrates the warning Jesus had just given about the Kingdom coming at a time that is currently unknown. Half of them were ready, and half were not, with very profound consequences."

"And the natural question for Matthew's readers," interjected the Younger, as what the Elder was suggesting came into focus for him, "would be: what does it mean to be 'ready'? Because it appears that they were all waiting for the Kingdom, but only half got in."

The Elder nodded in agreement, looking over his glasses at the Younger. "And the next parable, the Talents[18], sheds some light on that question. Two of the servants take what the Master has given them, and use it for the Kingdom. The third servant recited a well-rehearsed excuse for doing nothing, but the Master saw it differently, and the third servant was excluded from the Kingdom."

"That's the other thing that keeps coming up," interrupted the Younger a second time, shaking his head. "The whole concept of hell, or the outer darkness, or the weeping and gnashing of teeth. I know there's a lot of debate about what 'hell' actually is, but one thing seems clear: whatever hell is, it's not good, and Jesus warns people about it constantly."

He paused to drink deeply of his coffee before adding, "Jesus gave a lot of 'you have heard it said, but I say' corrections to peoples' expectations. But not about the threat of hell. If anything, Jesus took it up a notch by suggesting that the Pharisees, the holy law-keeping heroes, were sons of hell."

The Elder acknowledged his friend's observation with a solemn look. "And that comment," he quietly added, "leads into the final parable: the Sheep and the Goats[19]. If there was any question in the minds of Jesus' listeners about what sort of 'Kingdom work' they should be investing themselves in, this parable paints a pretty clear picture. They were to care for the poor, the downtrodden, the sick, and those in prison. In other words, the very people that Jesus spent most of His time caring for during His earthly ministry. By the way, does the parable of the Sheep and the Goats remind you of how Jesus described His own mission at the beginning of His public ministry?"

The Younger made the connection almost instantly. "When Jesus quoted Isaiah 61 in the synagogue[20]," he exclaimed, a note of wonder and discovery in his voice. "And when He defended His ministry to John the Baptist's disciples when they weren't sure if He was really the Messiah[21]. His proof of Messiah-ship was to tell them 'the blind see, the deaf hear, the lame walk, and the good news is preached to the poor'."

"And the 'issues of justice', as your generation calls them," added the Elder, "includes the releasing of the oppressed and the prisoner. Whether it's poverty, the exploitation of the weak – economically, physically or sexually – or even caring for God's creation, it's all included in the ethics of the Kingdom."

The Younger straightened, as the clock on the wall reminded him of his own schedule for the day. "I need to get going," he said absently, finishing his coffee, "but I have one last quote from Ladd that caught my eye, and I'd like to hear your thoughts, even if just a quick comment."

> "The Kingdom of God has entered into dynamic conflict with the realm of Satan, and God's reign is to manifest its powers in history through the church. The Kingdom of God working through Jesus' disciples is to make an impact upon the world. When Jesus said that they were to be the light of the world and the salt of the earth (Matthew 5:13-14), he meant that the world was to feel the influence of God's Kingdom."[22]

As the Younger began gathering up his things, stowing them in his messenger bag, the Elder gazed at him curiously, trying to anticipate the question behind the Younger's request. "Are you asking whether or not Christians should be involved in attempting to effect political change?"

The Younger nodded, even as he stepped out of the kitchen to retrieve his jacket. "Jesus' ministry certainly had political and social implications," he called from the hall, "not unlike the Old Testament prophetic voices."

"And if we're in the 'family business'," replied the Elder, rising from the table and following his friend down the hallway, "then the issues of justice would be our Kingdom responsibility as well, whether it be poverty, human trafficking, ecology or abortion."

The Younger had already reached the front door, but at the Elder's last phrase, he paused and turned back, hand resting on the doorknob. "I wasn't expecting to hear abortion lumped in with justice issues, to be honest. Most of my friends and I are more focused on poverty and human trafficking, things like that."

The Elder leaned against the kitchen doorframe, hands in his pockets. "So the rights of the unborn are no longer a justice issue? There was a time when Christians took a very different view. Civil disobedience was applauded in churches, although fire-bombing abortion clinics was rightly rejected."

The Younger opened the front door, but continued to linger, although it was obvious that time was weighing on him. "Yeah, I remember hearing stories about that when I was growing up," he said reluctantly, obviously uncomfortable with this unexpected turn in their discussion. "But those just aren't the justice issues that people are passionate about now."

The Elder remained where he was, deep in thought, yet mindful of the Younger's schedule. "Well, when did that change, and *why*?" he asked finally, leaving the doorframe and coming to stand next to his friend. "I realize you need to leave, but allow me to suggest something to think about later: Is there a 'prophetic' element that speaks to social justice for those of us who claim allegiance to the Kingdom? Or do we take our cues for justice only from those *outside* the Kingdom? It concerns me when society dictates what constitutes a true 'issue of justice'. If I could design a bumper sticker for that, I think it would say: 'Beware of Trendy Justice'."

He smiled as he clapped the Younger gently on the shoulder. "Of course, there's always the words of Jesus: 'if the salt loses its saltiness, it is no longer good for anything, except to be thrown out'.[23] I don't wish to use that verse as a blunt instrument, but it *is* part of Jesus' ethical teaching in the Sermon on the Mount. There is some level of 'seasoning' that citizens of the Kingdom *should* bring to the world around us. I worry sometimes when our commitment to justice only mirrors what the world calls 'justice'."

The Younger laughed weakly, and then shook his head with a rueful smile. "In the words of the old parishioner in the little country church: 'Preacher, you done gone from preachin', and now yer meddlin'. But as usual, you've given me something new to wrestle with. Thanks."

His 'thanks' was slightly facetious, but as the Elder watched him sling the messenger bag over his shoulder and stride purposefully towards his car, he knew that the Younger meant it.

He's a remarkable young man, mused the Elder, watching through the screen door as the Younger's car backed into the street. *He's honest and humble enough to be open to changing his mind.*

Closing the front door and refastening the two dead-bolt locks, the Elder lingered for a moment, his eyes wandering again to the wedding day photograph hanging in its frame on the wall.

Re-entering the kitchen, he dawdled briefly, adding the now-empty coffee cups to his recycling bin. A man of well-established habits, he then returned the meat cleaver to its place above the stove, and replaced the salt-shaker next to its pepper-filled twin in the kitchen cabinet next to the sink.

Taking a deep breath, he gently but firmly closed the cabinet door and turned resolutely to face the open door of his bedroom, once shared but now a solitary retreat. Memories were evoked simply by the softness of her favorite sweater, of evenings by the fire during their many winters. The dress that he thought she looked especially beautiful wearing, and candlelit dinners that celebrated many milestones.

And as he'd promised the Younger, he fully embraced the moment as he resumed his healing yet nostalgically bittersweet task.

Kitchen Justice Notes

1. *The Presence of the Future*, 215-216 *(emphasis added)*
2. Ibid., 216
3. Matthew 3:8
4. *The Presence of the Future*, 296
5. Ibid., 292
6. Matthew 25:14-30, also in the *Parable of the Ten Minas* (Luke 19:11-27)
7. Matthew 25:31-46
8. Luke 10:25-37
9. Matthew 18:21-35
10. Matthew 21:28-32
11. *The Presence of the Future*, 205 – "In answer to the young man's question about inheriting eternal life (Mark 10:17), Jesus spoke of entering the Kingdom (10:23-24) and receiving eternal life (10:30) as though they were synonymous concepts."
12. Ibid., 268
13. Matthew 7:21
14. Matthew 6:9-15 (cf. Luke 11:4 – Luke does not include the phrase "for unless you forgive", but Luke's rendition of Jesus' words – "***for*** we forgive others" – makes a connection between receiving the Father's forgiveness, and forgiving others

15. James 2:14-26
16. Matthew 23
17. Matthew 25:1-13
18. Matthew 25:14-30 (see also the *Parable of the Ten Minas*, Luke 19:11-27)
19. Matthew 25:31-46
20. Luke 4:14-21 (original prophecy is found in Isaiah 61:1-11)
21. Matthew 11:2-5; Luke 7:18-22
22. *The Presence of the Future*, 303
23. Matthew 5:13

Further Conversations

1. Hebrews 10:14 says: "For by one sacrifice he *(Jesus)* had made perfect forever those who are being made holy." Like any great scriptural truth, this verse could be abused and become pretty much irrelevant/ ineffectual. As a group, brainstorm some potential misuses of Hebrews 10:14, and come up with practical ways of avoiding these pitfalls.

2. How hard is it for you to simply… *receive*? Can you identify why?

3. How do we balance the reality that we receive the Kingdom like a child (not depending on our personal works) and the plain teaching of the Parable of the Talents (Matthew 25:14-30): use what God gave you or find yourself outside the Kingdom? Without becoming either paranoid/fearful or legalistic/judgmental?

4. Which 'issue(s) of justice' would be an 'easy sell' in your setting? What issues seem to be Christian-only in their importance?

5. After discussing the previous question: without becoming obnoxious zealots, how do we as Christians deal with issues of justice that rub non-Christians the wrong way?

chapter Ten
good news

"It's a digital SLR camera body, eighteen mega-pixels, but the real score was the lenses that came with it," the Barista said enthusiastically, patting the camera bag bursting with the rest of her treasures. "When I first saw it offered on eBay, I couldn't believe it. My 'dream camera gear' package, and it was for sale!" Her laughter offered a bright and musical contrast to the cool and overcast day, as she handed the camera to the Elder.

It's a small world after all, mused the Younger, as he watched the Barista and the Elder eagerly comparing notes on her new camera package. They had been cutting across the park en route to their favorite pub, kicking at the first fallen leaves of autumn, when they chanced upon the Barista taking photographs of the old statues near the iron gates. *What were the odds that she'd be taking pictures outside our pub, just when we would arrive?*

"I didn't realize you were into photography," the Younger said, inserting himself into their animated conversation. While his comment was directed at the Elder, it was the Barista who answered first.

"Oh, I've always had this dream of becoming a professional photographer. That's why I'm taking classes at the college," she enthused. "But it's really hard to pay for school and get decent camera gear with the kind of money I make at the *Genesis*."

"Don't get me wrong; I love working there," she hastened to add, as the cool fall breeze teased her dark hair across her face. "But it's not easy to save enough money for this kind of gear."

The Elder, cradling her new purchase with practiced ease as he gave it an admiring appraisal, smiled as he caught the Younger's eye. "Oh, photography has been a hobby of mine for many years. Although," he turned his attention and comment back to the Barista, "I'm rather partial to my old Pentax K1000. I still have a darkroom in my basement, believe it or not. Fortunately for those of us who are hopeless relics, there is an old photography shop near my place that still sells black and white Ilford film for 33mm antiques like mine."

Although he would probably have denied it if anyone had asked, the Younger had been of the opinion that the picture-taking capabilities of his cellphone were more than adequate. Suddenly, with this chance encounter, he wasn't so sure anymore. And as the Barista and the Elder enthusiastically continued to 'talk shop', he had to admit that the array of gear the Barista had recently purchased was impressive.

The Elder returned the camera to the Barista, his body language reminiscent of transferring a newborn child back to its mother. "I'm hoping to get at least three or four years out of the camera body, before I have to upgrade it," she was explaining. "The real treasure, like I said," and she placed her hand almost reverently on the well-padded camera bag, "is all the lenses that came with it. You see the 100mm lens on the camera? Well, I've also got a second prime 50mm lens *and* an image-stabilizing 75-200mm zoom. Plus a speedlight and a really good tripod."

She finished her verbal inventory with a flourish, beaming at them both. The Younger's friends often described him as technology-obsessed, but on this occasion he could only smile and nod as if he understood what she was saying, which he clearly did not. The Elder, despite his preference for antiquated photographic methodology, seemed not only to comprehend, but was also nodding with enthusiastic approval.

"Lenses are the biggest investment a photographer can make," the Elder commented matter-of-factly, speaking to the Barista but for the benefit of the Younger. "Even when the camera body is eventually upgraded to something newer, 'the magic is in the glass', as they say. Good lenses can be used indefinitely."

The Barista nodded energetically. "I had to sell my car, my ski equipment, even my gaming system – everything but the ring!" Her hand stretched further out of the long black sleeve of her hoodie, as she waved her engagement ring in front of them. "These lenses alone usually cost about ten grand. It's a dream come true, but it wasn't cheap, not by a long shot. But totally worth it! My fiancé said to go for it, before somebody else did."

Her enthusiasm was infectious; by now, both of her listeners were smiling almost as widely as she was. The Elder tipped his cap as he commented, "I'm sure you'll enjoy many years with these lenses. And with your passion for photography, I'm certain it will only be a matter of time before we start seeing your work on display around town."

The Elder's gracious blessing caught her off-guard; for a moment, she simply stared blankly at him, uncharacteristically silent. "Thank you," she quietly said at last. "That was very kind of you to say."

The vulnerable moment passed, and as her typical enthusiasm and energy re-asserted itself, she lifted her camera into the ready position. "How about a picture of the two of you?" she offered cheerfully.

They glanced at each other, and by wordless mutual consent, attempted to strike a casual pose. The Barista clicked several shots in rapid succession, and lowered the camera to check her handiwork on the digital screen of the camera. "Not bad," she commented. "I can email you copies, unless either of you has a flash drive on you."

The Elder opened his mouth as if to answer, but the Younger took matters into his own hands, digging into an inner pocket of his jacket and pulling out his business card. The Barista accepted it, balancing the camera against her shoulder with her other hand as she read the information on the card. "Okay, no problem. I'll email these to you probably later tonight."

And then with a cheerful wave and one last beaming smile, she set off towards the far end of the small urban park, pausing now and then to take more photographs as the trees, statues, and iron fences captured her imagination. The Elder turned, hands in his pockets, as he gently reprimanded the Younger. "I *do* have an email address, you know. I even check it, every now and then."

The Younger shrugged helplessly, as they both resumed their steps towards the pub. "Sorry, but it was an honest mistake. You're the one who insists on just having a landline, after all. You might be the only person I know who doesn't own a cellphone. How do people ever track you down?"

"I'm not a dinosaur," protested the Elder, shaking his finger at the Younger. "I have an answering machine, too. Right next to the toaster oven."

The Younger couldn't decide if his friend was being facetious or not, so he chose the better part of valor and changed the subject. "I don't think she was expecting you to say what you did," he commented as he pulled open the heavy wooden door, holding it ajar for the Elder to enter. "It's amazing how much impact even a simple compliment can have on someone."

"As Mark Twain once said, 'I can live for two months on a good compliment'. The gift of encouragement is something of a lost art," agreed the Elder, as they entered the pub. With barely a pause inside the entrance, they automatically headed for their traditional booth, its window overlooking the park they had just taken their shortcut through. "And she also encourages me; she's something of a 'living parable'."

"You mean losing her ring and then finding it again?" offered the Younger, as he reached over to adjust the window blind, allowing as much of the late-afternoon light as possible into their booth. "I finally figured out what you were talking about, the last time we were at the *Genesis*. She's the Parable of the Lost Coin, isn't she?"

The door opened abruptly behind them as the Proprietress entered the building, her confident strides faltering only slightly as she caught sight of the familiar pair in the corner booth. Her momentary hesitation quickly passed, and with slightly raised eyebrows and a resigned sigh, she resumed her determined steps into the office behind the bar.

The Barkeep, having already noted their presence when they first arrived, was preemptively drawing a pair of pints as his wife swept by. The amber ale for the Younger sat prepped and ready, and the Elder's pint was being given careful attention. *You never draw Guinness in a hurry*, the Barkeep thought, recalling the strict instruction of his mentor, all those years ago in Dublin. *Might be I should ask m'lady to get some curry fries started, just in case.*

The Elder emptied most of his satchel's contents onto the table: *Jesus and the Kingdom*, his battered old Bible, and a spiral-bound notebook. The Younger's e-reader, by contrast, took up far less real estate in their booth. "Absolutely yes," he began, in answer to the Younger's earlier question. "Our friend the Barista is a modern parable of the Lost Coin. And in the park just now, she was a second parable as well."

"The Treasure Hidden in a Field!" exclaimed the Younger instantly, as he shucked off his jacket. "Or maybe the Pearl of Great Price. How am I doing?"

Laughing, the Elder gave a small, exaggerated cheer. Neither of them saw the immediate reaction of the concerned Proprietress, her head popping up from behind the bar like a startled prairie dog.

"The parallels are striking, you must admit," the Elder continued, more seriously. "I was tempted to say to her, 'the Kingdom is near'. We might have had a good conversation about how she is a living parable of Jesus."

"Or you might have scared her away!" countered the Younger, laughing nervously. "Sometimes I think the only thing we're really good at in 'evangelism' is giving people a new pet peeve about Christianity."

The Elder concurred, although with some reservation. "It really depends on relationship, or 'earning the right to be heard', if you will.

"Think about it, though: we've connected over her story of finding her lost engagement ring, we've had a pleasant conversation with her about camera gear, and she's going to be sending us copies of the pictures she took. And..." he paused for emphasis, "since we frequent *The Genesis Café* quite regularly, we'll be continuing to interact with her, 'earning the right to be heard'."

The Barkeep entered their peripheral view at that moment, a pint clasped in each of his strong hands, Guinness to the Elder, and the IPA to the Younger. "Anything to eat this fine afternoon, gents?" he asked, his Irish accent as strong and pure as the day he'd emigrated. "Curry fries, if I might wager a guess?"

The Younger nodded in enthusiastic agreement, but the Elder surprised everyone by breaking from tradition. "I'm thinking about Shepherd's Pie, actually," he said, folding his hands on the table as he looked up at the Barkeep, who despite his average height, seemed to tower over them. *I'll bet he was a force to be reckoned with on the soccer pitch*, the Elder thought.

"Shepherd's Pie, and a plate o' curry fries," amended the Barkeep, scarcely missing a beat. And he turned on his heel, heading back to his waiting wife at the bar.

The Younger leaned forward to whisper conspiratorially, "I'd be willing to bet that 'earning the right to be heard' might be a little more daunting with our Crusty Irish Barkeep."

The Elder acknowledged his comment with a noncommittal shrug. "Perhaps. Sometimes, I'm surprised when people I'd assumed were disinterested actually turned out to be quite open to discussing spiritual matters. And the opposite can also be true, as well. You never know until you try."

Turning back to his pile of books, he continued, "And you're touching on a very important topic. We've already invested a good deal of time exploring different aspects of the Kingdom: what people's expectations of the Kingdom were, how Jesus interpreted the already-and-not-yet Kingdom in Himself and His ministry, and the ethics of the Kingdom. This should lead us quite naturally to the next question in our understanding of the Kingdom."

The Younger interrupted quietly but with uncharacteristic firmness. "What does 'the Kingdom is near, repent and believe the good news' mean for us today." It was a statement, more than a question. "I'll be honest: this is something I've wrestled with – how exactly is the Gospel 'good news' in our day and age?"

He collected his e-reader from the table top, bringing its screen to life. "Personally, it was helpful when Ladd reminded me of the spiritual dynamic of the Kingdom. Aside from the obvious, I mean, that the Kingdom *is* a spiritual reality. Listen to this:

> "The chief opponents of God's Kingdom are spiritual and the victory of the kingdom of God is first of all a spiritual victory."[1]
>
> "The exorcism of demons was one of the most characteristic activities of Jesus' ministry. At the very outset, Mark strikes the note of exorcism as one of the motifs of Jesus' ministry (Mark 1:23-28). The mission of the twelve (Mark 6:7) and of the seventy as well (Luke 10:17) emphasizes this same motif."[2]

The Younger lowered his e-reader and looked the Elder squarely in the eye. “I know this should be obvious, but in all the discussions I’ve had with friends about justice, ethics, culture, and faith... Well, to be brutally honest, somehow we overlooked the whole ‘kingdoms in conflict’ aspect of the Kingdom. It’s as if we forgot that we’re in a spiritual battle. At times, I wonder if – unintentionally, of course – we’ve only succeeded in bringing the Kingdom down to our level, where we can manage it ourselves.”

The Elder listened respectfully, his expression kind but concerned. “Well, as Solomon observed quite some time ago: ‘there is nothing new under the sun’. The Sadducees, if you recall, were some of Jesus’ biggest critics, and they didn’t believe in a supernatural realm either, or a world beyond this one. Jesus’ concept of the Kingdom coming ‘apocalyptically’ would have been completely unacceptable to them. Their view of the Kingdom was entirely political and this-worldly, because they didn’t believe there *was* anything beyond this life.”

The Younger nodded, straightening in his chair as he warmed to the discussion. “And all through the gospels, and the Acts of the Apostles, the whole ‘kingdoms in conflict’ theme is repeated over and over again. You’d have to deliberately ignore a lot of Scripture to miss it.”

Switching applications on his e-reader, the Younger continued, “I mean, the first time Jesus sends out the twelve disciples to ‘preach the good news’, He specifically includes healing the sick and casting out demons[3]. And when He sends out the seventy-two for the same reason, even though He didn't mention demons, the disciples came back very excited because they'd had power over demons in His name."[4]

"Ah, that reminds me of something else Ladd wrote," the Elder concurred, pausing to enjoy some of his Guinness before quoting from *Jesus and the Kingdom* once again:

> **"The Kingdom is God's dynamic power, and it must 'come' because there are real spiritual enemies which oppose it, both human and super-human. The 'coming' of God's Kingdom means the invasion of the power of Satan and the overthrow of his kingdom."[5]**

The Elder looked up from his reading, peering over the rims of his glasses. "You said something earlier along these same lines, I believe. The 'issues of justice' are both actions that we take in the here-and-now, as well as a form of spiritual warfare."

The Elder eagerly switched to his Bible as he picked up steam. "What I find significant and encouraging, since you mentioned Jesus sending out the disciples," he enthused as he located the passage he was looking for, "is the widening circle of who was commissioned to spread the Message of the Kingdom.

"At first, it was the twelve, then the seventy-two, and after Pentecost, everyone who is filled with the Holy Spirit is therefore equipped to be witnesses of Jesus the Messiah."

Ahem, the Proprietress interrupted, clearing her throat to draw their attention. Looking up, the two conversationalists belatedly realized that she was standing there, steaming plates held in her hands. As they quickly cleared some space on the table, she placed their meals before them, and with a studiously neutral expression on her face, retreated at speed to the bar.

"Fanatics," she muttered to the Barkeep, shaking her head. "All they ever talk about is religion."

The Barkeep studied them for a moment, as they continued in their animated conversation, juggling books, electronic devices, and their forks. "Any weapons tonight?"

His wife shook her head: no. "Ah, let 'em talk," he advised under his breath, as he continued to draw pints for another table full of customers. "As long as they dinnae bother nobody else."

Meanwhile, back at the table, the conversation continued unabated.

"There were, if you look at it in a certain way, *three* Pentecosts," the Elder was saying, turning pages with his left hand, as he industriously stirred his shepherd's pie into a single concoction with the other. "First, the one recorded in the second chapter of Acts during the actual Feast of Pentecost[6], where observant Jews from around the known world were gathered.

"The second, in Acts chapter eight, was with the despised mixed-race Samaritans[7], and the third Pentecost occurred among an uncouth, non-kosher Gentile audience in chapter ten[8]. I'd like to suggest that, just as the circle of who participates in the spread of the Kingdom was expanding, so too is the circle of who can be included in the Kingdom."

"Even the Ethiopian eunuch's conversion[9] was a fulfillment of an Old Testament prophecy[10], where the Father promised to include foreigners and eunuchs in His Kingdom. Both groups were once seen as 'outsiders' to God's covenant people." The Elder was as animated as the Younger had ever seen him; clearly, this topic was one near and dear to his heart. The Younger felt a similar thrill of anticipation as they continued their conversation.

"The point I'm trying to make is simply this," the Elder smiled as he concluded. "The gospel of the Kingdom began to reach all people groups within just a short period of time. By pouring out the Holy Spirit on the Samaritans and Gentiles, God was making it clear that the Kingdom would include anyone who believed and repented."

Sensing that they'd reached a conclusion of sorts, the Younger switched applications once again, calling up another set of notes he'd written.

"There are two conversations listed in the Bible that I really wish I could have heard in person," he began. "Or, at least, it would have been helpful if the content of those conversations had been written down."

Referring to his notes, he continued, "First, what did Jesus *actually say* to the disciples on the road to Emmaus[11]? That time when he 'opened up the Scriptures' (meaning, the Old Testament), and explained how everything pointed to Him."

"And the other?" prompted the Elder, his fork suspended in mid-air.

"After the resurrection," exclaimed the Younger, gathering momentum, "where it says, 'He appeared to them over a period of forty days and spoke about the kingdom of God.'[12] Did you catch that? *Forty days* of Jesus teaching about the Kingdom, with the additional motivation of listening to someone who had just been *raised from the dead."* The Younger paused for breath, shaking his head in amazement. "I would have loved to have been there, to hear exactly what Jesus taught them about the Kingdom. So many of the questions I have about the 'gospel of the Kingdom' for today could have been answered. I can't believe no-one thought to write anything down!"

The Elder finished his meal, wiping his hands on a napkin and pushing his plate – knife and fork neatly arranged at the 'four o'clock' position – to the outside edge of the table.

"To answer to your Emmaus road question," he shrugged with a short, self-deprecating laugh, "I have absolutely no idea. The Bible doesn't say one way or the other. However, remember that Jesus often spoke in parables, which required people to think a little harder and dig a little deeper. It's a possibility that the Emmaus Road record deliberately didn't include an easy-to-follow, step-by-step explanation."

He raised his hands in a cautionary gesture. "Now, that's just a theory, of course. But if it motivates us to study the Old Testament more often, that's probably a good thing in the long run."

"And?" prompted the Younger, as he cleaned the last of the curry fries from his plate and pushed it aside. "The part about forty days of Kingdom teaching with Jesus that nobody wrote down?"

The Elder shifted in his chair as he pulled his Bible closer. "Truth be told," he submitted, "I think we *do* have a pretty good idea of what Jesus taught the disciples during that time. Remember, He'd already given them the Great Commission[13], to make disciples, and He had also instructed them to wait in Jerusalem for the 'promise of the Father': the Holy Spirit[14]."

The Proprietress materialized at table's edge, deftly collecting the Elder's plate. Turning to the Younger, she asked, abruptly but not unkindly, "Are you finished?"

"Oh, yes, of course," stumbled the Younger, hastening to hand his empty plate and utensils to her. As she moved away, he looked at the Elder, uncomprehending. "She asks me if I'm done, but somehow, she just knows you're finished. What's the deal with where you put your cutlery on your plate?"

The Elder smiled benignly in response. "You are too far removed from the 'Old Country' traditions," he teased. "Perhaps you should 'Google it' when you get home."

The Younger shook his head, recovering quickly, all business as he returned to the topic at hand. "So, help me understand: what's your theory on the actual content of those forty days of teaching about the Kingdom?"

"Ah yes," concurred the Elder, spreading out his books and notes over the extra space now available on the table. "We have written records in the *Acts of the Apostles* of what the disciples actually said when they had the opportunity to 'preach the Kingdom'. And each of these opportunities took place in several unique locations, each with differing speakers and differing audiences. I can't absolutely prove this, of course, but I would like to suggest that what the disciples said, when given the opportunity, comes directly from what Jesus taught them in preparation for the outpouring of the Holy Spirit."

The Younger looked pensive as he considered this, but then a slow grin spread across his face as he met the gaze of the Elder. "Why do I get the feeling you've already thought about this, and came prepared?" he asked, gesturing to the Elder's spiral-bound notebook. "I've never seen you bring this notebook before."

The Elder motioned for the Proprietress, as he feigned innocence. "Why do you ask? Do you find it shocking that I may have actually given this some thought before, at some point in my many long years of life?"

They ordered coffee as the Proprietress swept by, empty drink tray in one hand.

"To be honest," the Elder confided, as he rotated his notebook so that the Younger could see what he'd drawn in its pages, "not only have I given some thought to the

Gospel of the Kingdom beforehand, I've also created a chart showing the specific content from each recorded sermon that the early disciples preached." *(See Appendix: Gospel of the Kingdom in Acts)*

"Could I take this home with me?" inquired the Younger, impressed as he perused the neat lines of hand-written notations, the markings in blue ink smudged here and there. "I'd like to re-do this in digital form for future reference. Or at least scan it."

"By all means," replied the Elder, leaning back in his chair to make way as their coffees arrived, deftly placed on the table by the Proprietress, with a small metal pitcher of cream between them.

As she continued on her way, a whirling dervish of efficiency, the Elder returned to his former position, elbows on table. "I would like to pose a question: If we truly wish to understand what the 'gospel of the Kingdom' is for our present day, does it not make sense to explore how the first disciples understood it? They preached it everywhere, as they moved from Jerusalem, to Samaria, and ultimately to Rome, the center of the known world at that time. The key question would be: what content did *they* feel compelled to include? And was the content the same for each audience: Jew, Samaritan, and Gentile?"

The Younger pulled the Elder's notes closer as he continued to read. "That makes a lot of sense," he concurred, eyes roving over the page. "Especially if your theory about what Jesus taught during those forty days turns out to be correct."

"Any observations? What common elements do you see in how the 'good news of the Kingdom' was proclaimed?" prodded the Elder, gesturing towards the hand-written chart he'd created.

The Younger looked up from the notebook, a familiar mischievous expression in his lop-sided smile. "Well, I can see that St. Peter had a lot to learn about being 'seeker-sensitive', for starters. Whenever he speaks to his own people – including the religious leaders – he almost always starts with 'you killed the Messiah'."

The Elder laughed, shaking his head. "Even before being filled with the Holy Spirit, Peter did have a tendency to speak boldly. But I would also hasten to point out that Peter stresses: (a) Jesus is the promised Messiah they'd all been waiting for, (b) yes, as you said, the Jews killed Him, but also (c) that God vindicated Jesus as the Messiah by raising Him from the dead."

"Peter also seems to expect that their most reasonable response would be to repent," observed the Younger, referring again to the notebook before him. "At least, that's his conclusion when speaking to his countrymen[15]. And I see that Peter includes the promise of having their sins forgiven, and receiving the gift of the Holy Spirit, if they believe and repent."

The Elder continued to lean on his elbows, craning his neck as he read the chart upside down. "And you can see that Peter says almost exactly the same thing when he and John are being questioned by the Sanhedrin, the spiritual leaders of Israel. In fact, Peter tells them the same thing, *twice*: Jesus is the Messiah; you killed Him but God raised Him from the dead; forgiveness of sins and the gift of the Spirit come through Him. Peter is certainly a different man than the coward who denied Jesus three times[16] just a few weeks earlier."

The Younger pointed to a longer section of the list: Stephen's speech[17] in front of the same Sanhedrin that had earlier questioned and threatened Peter and John[18]. "I notice that Stephen dared to lecture the spiritual leaders on their own history, and went even further by saying that the leaders were no different than those who abandoned God to worship the Golden Calf. And, like Peter, he was pretty specific: 'you betrayed and murdered Him'[19], although I suspect it was Stephen saying that he saw a vision of Jesus at the right hand of God that pushed them over the edge."[20]

"They were losing control, and I don't mean just of their tempers," agreed the Elder, suddenly somber. "They had crucified Jesus, and thought their problems were over. Then came the resurrection, which they tried to cover up.[21] Later, to make things even worse, miracles continue to happen, and the disciples are boldly telling everyone Jesus is the Messiah, raised from the dead by the power of God. All of this would make the religious leaders look very, very bad in the eyes of the people. Perhaps it's not all that surprising that this would eventually boil over into the murder of Stephen, followed immediately by the active persecution of Jesus' followers."[22]

The Younger finished off his coffee in a single, prolonged draft, although on this particular evening, the coffee had cooled enough that he had no immediate regrets. The Elder turned to signal the Proprietress, but she was already en route to their table, coffee carafe in hand. *It's nice to be in a place with such attentive service,* marveled the Elder, never suspecting the real reason behind the Proprietress' watchful eye on their table.

Their cups replenished, the Younger poured cream into his own mug, while the Elder carefully wiped away the circle of condensation on the table left behind by the metal cream pitcher. "Do you notice any differences in Peter's message when he's speaking to a non-Jewish audience?" he asked, frowning at the dampness on the table, so close to his precious books.

The Younger took a cautious sip before replying. The coffee, hot and with a dusky aroma, added a welcome familiarity to their conversation. "No, not that I can see, except that he says 'they' killed Jesus, instead of 'you'." He looked up with a grin. "That probably helped improve his audience's attitudes."

"But beyond that, it's the same," he continued, setting his coffee mug on the table. "Jesus is the Messiah, God raised Him from the dead, forgiveness and the Holy Spirit are promised to those who believe. And then all of them were baptized."

"And the Jewish believers who came with Peter were amazed that Gentiles were now included in the Kingdom," added the Elder. "The gift of the Holy Spirit was the 'proof of the pudding', if you will. Some of the other Jewish believers in Jerusalem, however, later accused Peter of breaking Jewish law by entering a Gentile's house[23]. And all that was required to change their minds was hearing about Peter's vision, and that the Holy Spirit had been given to the Gentiles who believed[24]. Such a quick change of heart is something of a minor miracle in itself," he concluded with a chuckle.

The Younger sipped his coffee as his eyes wandered over the second part of the Elder's chart. "Here's something else," he commented. "I never noticed before how similar Paul's sermon is to Stephen's and Peter's. The same history lesson – even though he's speaking to a synagogue crowd, whom you'd think would know their own history – and how the Resurrection is 'proof' that Jesus really is the promised Messiah."

The Elder reached over to point out another line. "And like Peter, Paul specifically mentions Jesus forgiving our sins, which the Law of Moses could not. That kind of forgiveness was only possible if Jesus was the Messiah. Hence the reason that Peter, Stephen, and Paul take care to show how Jesus fulfills the Old Testament, by reminding them of their story, their history."

The Elder rotated his notebook halfway, allowing each of them to look at the handwritten chart more easily. "And in another synagogue, in Thessalonica, Paul is recorded as 'proving from the Scriptures' that the Messiah had to suffer, as well as the significance of the Resurrection, and that Jesus of Nazareth was the Messiah[25]. There is clearly a pattern in how the disciples understood and proclaimed 'the gospel of the Kingdom'."

The Younger frowned at the second last item on the Elder's chart, running his finger along the neat lines that the Elder had written. "And even though Paul chooses a different way of saying things when he's talking to the philosophers in Athens, I see that he still hits most of the same points: the need for repentance, the resurrection of Jesus, and a day of judgment – or separation – that is coming in the future."[26]

The Elder finished his second coffee, sliding the mug over next to the condiments, as he summed up the next and final reference in his notebook chart. "What I find fascinating is that Paul gives something of his own personal story – his 'testimony' – and uses that as a springboard to proclaim the Kingdom. It's the first recorded instance of someone including his or her story as part of the Kingdom message. Paul then goes on to cover much of the same ground as before: that Jesus is the Messiah, and how the Old Testament foretold that the Messiah would suffer and die (which always surprised anyone hoping for a political Messiah), and be raised from the dead."[27]

"Hey, I just noticed this," exclaimed the Younger, double-checking the Elder's final notebook entry against his e-reader. "Paul's message is 'repent', and – to use John the Baptist's words – 'produce fruit of repentance'. There is definitely a pattern, from John the Baptist preaching in the wilderness, Jesus' teachings, and the apostles spreading the gospel of the Kingdom."

The Elder glanced at his watch, and began to gather his things together, turning to pull his satchel closer. The

Younger, likewise noting the time in the top corner of his e-reader, also reached for his messenger bag.

"There's something else that Paul mentions," added the Elder, as he neatly arranged his belongings in the satchel, although leaving his copy of Ladd on the table, "which brings us full circle to the beginning of this conversation. There are two kingdoms in conflict. Paul claimed that 'God said' that he was to proclaim the message of Jesus, to turn people from Satan's power to God's, so that their sins could be forgiven."[28]

"And last, but certainly not least," he concluded, indicating *Jesus and the Kingdom*, "the common element throughout the teachings of Jesus, and the spread of the 'good news of the Kingdom' in Acts, is the need to make a decision. We've only just begun to scratch the surface, to be honest, but why don't we give George Ladd the last word for this evening:"

> "Men cannot passively await the coming of the eschatological Kingdom as the apocalyptists taught. On the contrary, the Kingdom has come to them, and they are actively, aggressively, forcefully to seize it."[29]

"And the forceful ones lay hold of it," quoted the Younger with a nod, recalling the insights from the last time they'd been discussing the Kingdom in the pub. Frowning suddenly, he ventured another question as the thought occurred to him. "Getting back to the gospel of the Kingdom for today, how do you just go up to somebody and say, 'the Kingdom is near, repent and believe that Jesus is the Messiah? And He will forgive your sins, and give you the Holy Spirit'?

"Most of the people I know would be incredibly offended if you suggested that any of their actions or attitudes could be called 'sinful'. I'd be labeled and dismissed as an irrelevant bigot," he concluded darkly, feeling overwhelmed.

The Elder sighed. "You told me the other day that I'd gone from preachin' and started meddlin'," he said carefully, attempting to lighten the Younger's mood.

"If you don't mind, I think I'll continue in that fine tradition by quoting Jesus: 'It is not the healthy who need a doctor, but the sick. I have not come to call the righteous, but sinners.'"[30]

Leaning on the table once more, choosing his words carefully, the Elder continued.

"Jesus spoke these words to the Pharisees, because they refused to see their own need, and were offended that Jesus was offering the Kingdom to people they found unworthy. This may sound pretentious, although I certainly don't intend it that way, but isn't it ironic that the attitude of the Pharisees – 'there's nothing wrong with me' – is mirrored by much of our society today?"

Leaning back in his chair, the Elder continued quietly, "Perhaps that is why, to this very day, the gospel of the Kingdom finds its most receptive audience among the poor, the oppressed, and any others who recognize and admit their need."

The Younger looked thoughtful, but the expression on his face told the Elder that he would be thinking long and hard between this evening and their next time together. "I had underlined this quote from Ladd already," he said slowly, "but now it makes even more sense:"

> "Jesus must bring the saving good news of the Kingdom to such sinners. He does not deny that they are sinners, nor does he make light of their guilt. Rather he points to their need and ministers to it."[31]

"I guess it goes back to the Parable of the Sower," concluded the Younger, standing up from the table. "We sow the seed, and depending on the condition of the soil..." his voiced trailed off.

"But the seed is still the dynamic power of God," the Elder reminded him, also rising from his side of the booth. "And the God who comes is still the seeking God who draws people to Himself by His Spirit. That's why 'earning the right to be heard' is so important."

As they began to pull their jackets on, the Proprietress suddenly appeared at their table. With an air of unquestioned authority, she produced their bill, placing it on the table between them like a gauntlet of challenge.

My, the service here certainly is attentive, thought the Elder for the second time, just before his eyes chanced on the total at the bottom of the bill. The Younger noticed the sum at the same time, and snatched up the bill to examine it more closely, his expression one of shock and disbelief.

Lifting their incredulous gaze from the unexpected sum, they noticed for the first time, just behind the Proprietress, the presence of the Barkeep. "You dinnae pay yer bill last time," observed the Barkeep in a no-nonsense tone of voice, wiping his burly hands on his omnipresent towel. The Proprietress waited silently, arms crossed as her husband continued. "And I figured two men o' the cloth might want to make amends."

The Younger's gaze made guilty contact with the Elder's, as the two of them recognized the truth in the Barkeep's words. They were so shocked that neither of them even thought to explain that they weren't clergy. They quickly settled the debt, and the Elder made a point of leaving a sizable tip.

"To use your old quote: 'Good lord and butter'," observed the Younger, exhaling a deep breath as they found themselves outside on the sidewalk. The heavy wooden door swung shut behind them with a dull thud of finality. "So much for 'earning the right to be heard', eh?"

The Elder shook his head, still somewhat red-faced in embarrassment. Then, rallying himself, he straightened his shoulders as he responded to the Younger's comment. "No, there is yet hope," he promised, beginning to regain his usual good humor.

He adjusted his cap, echoing the Younger's heavy sigh. "It may just take a little longer."

Good News Notes

1. *The Presence of the Future*, 151
2. Ibid., 149
3. Luke 9:1-6
4. Luke 10:1-11, 17-20
5. *The Presence of the Future*, 155
6. Acts 2:1-41
7. Acts 8:5-8, 14-17
8. Acts 10:24-48
9. Acts 8:26-40
10. Isaiah 56:3-8
11. Luke 24:13-35
12. Acts 1:3
13. Matthew 28:18-20
14. Acts 1:4-8
15. Acts 2:14-41; 3:11-26
16. Matthew 26:69-75; Mark 14:66-72; Luke 22:54-62; John 18:15-18, 25-27
17. Acts 7:1-53
18. Acts 4:21, 5:40
19. Acts 7:52-54
20. Acts 7:55-60

21. Matthew 28:11-15
22. Acts 8:1-3
23. Acts 11:1-3
24. Acts 11:4-18
25. Acts 17:1-4
26. Acts 17:22-32
27. Acts 26:1-23
28. Acts 26:15-18
29. *The Presence of the Future*, 164
30. Matthew 9:12-13, Mark 2:17, Luke 5:30-32
31. *The Presence of the Future*, 175

Further Conversations

1. Imagine yourself in your favorite café/pub. Now picture yourself approaching someone you recognize at a nearby table and saying, "the Kingdom is near". How *do* we initiate conversations about the 'good news'?
2. Agree/Disagree: "Before you can get them 'found', you have to get them 'lost'." Why/why not?
3. Stop for a moment and reflect on how *you* came to faith in Jesus. Share your stories as a group, paying special attention to the question: What was it that made you receptive to the message of the Gospel, instead of reactive against it? When/how did that change?
4. Earlier, we looked at spiritual warfare as a part of the issues of justice. When Jesus sent out His disciples to 'preach the good news of the kingdom' (Luke 9 & 10), He gave them authority over demonic spirits. How might this shape our understanding of sharing our faith with friends and family?
5. Check out the *Gospel of the Kingdom in Acts* in the Appendices. As a group, brainstorm how you would put the various elements of the Message into your own words. Do this with specific friends/family in mind (to keep it real and not hypothetical).

Extra Credit

1. Begin praying for the friends/family that you had in mind (don't forget the spiritual warfare part). Keep praying until the opportunity to share the Message comes (it will!).
2. Ponder/discuss: if the poor and oppressed have always been (a) a major focus of Jesus' ministry, and (b) the most receptive to the Gospel of the Kingdom, what does that suggest about where and with whom we should invest our time and energy?

chapter Eleven
coffee & toast

What a mess, I thought, marveling at the worn and disheveled appearance of my journal. Several months' worth of reading, research and reflection had clearly taken its toll. In a way, the journal served as a symbolic reflection for our journey through Ladd and the Kingdom of God: page after page of notes, margins crammed with scribbled notes about the notes, yellow highlighting of key thoughts, and arrows crisscrossing every which way between all of the above.

Tucked into the inside cover were numerous printouts of the summaries that the Younger had faithfully emailed to me after each of their conversations. The printouts had fared little better than the rest of the journal: marked, underlined, and cross-referenced.

Out of the corner of my eye, I was aware that the Younger and the Elder were getting reacquainted with the Barista as they ordered their beverages. Their cheerful and animated voices were noticeable above the usual ambient buzz of conversation in the café, although not distinct enough to pick out what they were saying.

Only moments before, they had greeted me in equally boisterous fashion as they arrived. *It never even occurs to them that they're consistently just a little late,* I thought with some amusement. *They definitely march to the beat of their own drum.*

I was enjoying another taste of my *americano* when the Younger and Elder joined me at the window-side table; the same coveted table I had narrowly missed acquiring during our previous visit.

"Welcome to my favorite window perch," I greeted them, gesturing to the view overlooking the tree-lined street, its cobblestone sidewalks bustling with pedestrians in the late afternoon sun.

"Everyone has his or her own 'happy place'," quipped the Younger, looping the strap of his messenger bag over the back of his chair and pulling out his e-reader with practiced ease. "But I can see why this one appeals to you."

The Elder, having placed his steaming cup of black coffee on the table, busied himself with extracting various books from his worn leather satchel.

Arranging the books meticulously next to his coffee, he ended his flurry of activity by squeezing the satchel into what little space remained between his chair and the wall of the café.

"And the advantage of coming to this particular café," he observed, pausing to drink some of his coffee, "is that we are given the opportunity of paying at the counter when we order our drinks." Indicating the cash register by the espresso bar, he continued, "Thus are we spared later humiliation at the hands of the proprietors."

The Younger groaned audibly at the memory, burying his face in his hands. I chose to drink more of my *americano* at that moment, and kept any facetious remarks to myself.

The Elder removed his reading glasses from an inner pocket in his jacket, perching them on his nose, an obvious prelude to our anticipated discussion.

The Younger responded to the non-verbal cue by powering up his e-reader, while I flipped open my copy of Ladd to one of its many bookmarks.

On second thought, I decided to put my open journal on top of *The Presence of the Future*.

"Now, where were we?" the Younger intoned, equal parts mischief and seriousness, as was typical for him. "You're the writer," he added, pointing at me with his latte. "Where do you want to start today?"

I fidgeted absent-mindedly with the corner of my journal's denim cover as I answered his question. "I took the bus downtown today, so I had some extra time to skim through a lot of my notes on the way here.

"I know it feels like we've barely scratched the surface on the Kingdom of God, but as I review what we've discussed, we really have covered a great deal of material in a fairly short amount of time."

Glancing down at the journal, I pointed out the list I'd started a few minutes earlier, just before their arrival. "I'm thinking of things like the expectations of the people when Jesus first arrived. And how Jesus didn't *refute* their views as much as He *re-defined* God's role: in history, in the future Kingdom to come, and even the ethical and justice aspects of the Kingdom."

The Younger began to chuckle quietly, and I looked up in time to see the Elder quietly, and with solemn ceremony, retrieve several small items from his satchel.

Unhurried, he carefully arranged them in the middle of the table: a small bottle of *salsa picante*, a funny-looking saltshaker that was shaped like a hamburger, and a tiny little two-pronged pickle fork.

Sensing that all eyes were on him, the Elder hastened to explain. "I wanted to include visual reminders of our discussions, but I thought it would be very unwise to repeat my earlier mistake of bringing a meat cleaver into such a public setting."

"Yes, he can be taught!" I announced facetiously, thankful for the progressive substitutions in kitchen utensils as metaphors.

The Younger scooped up the pickle fork and brandished it, alert for any alarmed response. Unlike their previous experience with the meat cleaver, the pickle fork evoked absolutely zero reaction, either from nearby patrons or from the Barista. "The Pickle Fork of the Apocalypse," he mused, skeptical. "I don't know. It just doesn't have the same aura of menace. I'll just look at it as a symbol of the symbol of the real thing."

I pulled out my copy of Ladd from beneath my journal, as the Younger replaced the pickle fork on the table, next to the other symbolic kitchen items. "Something that we've touched on before," I began, smoothing the page with my fingers, "but I really think needs mentioning again, is this:

> **"Furthermore, the Kingdom is something which is to be received here and now (Mark 10:15, Luke 18:17, Matthew 18:3). What must be received is not a realm, present or future, but a reign, God's reign, and the blessings which accompany it. To receive the Kingdom of God is to accept the yoke of God's sovereignty."[1]**

The Younger spoke up as I finished reading. "I've been thinking about that, as well. When I was 'young and foolish', I assumed the gospel of the Kingdom was mostly just spiritual 'fire insurance' and going to heaven when I die. One of the things on my short list of *Stuff I've Learned From Ladd* would have to be that the Kingdom is not a place, it's a relationship with the King and His purposes in history, *right now*."

The Elder had been listening quietly to the Younger and me, but now he folded his hands on the table and added his own comments. "I've had the opportunity to read Ladd more than once, during several different seasons in my life. Although, to be honest, it's been some time since I last read anything by him. Personally, I've very much enjoyed, and been challenged again, by revisiting my theological roots."

Glancing down at his copy of Ladd, the Elder reached absent-mindedly into an inner pocket of his jacket to retrieve his reading glasses.

There was a brief moment of consternation, until he realized belatedly that he was already wearing them, but he continued his thought as if nothing had happened. "And in revisiting my roots, I am reminded of an old song: 'this world is not my home, I'm just passing through'. We discover our true identity when we enter the already-and-not-yet Kingdom; we receive a new citizenship. May I?" he concluded, indicating his copy of Ladd.

Intrigued and curious, the Younger and I immediately nodded our agreement. The Elder adjusted his glasses, ran his finger quickly down the page to the quote he was looking for, and then read aloud with a quiet but impassioned tone:

> "The Kingdom of God has entered into dynamic conflict with the realm of Satan, and God's reign is to manifest its powers in history through the church."[2]

"And this second quote," the Elder continued, scarcely looking up, "which relates to the first:

> "The church, as it has often been said, is a people who live 'between the times'. They are caught up in a tension between the Kingdom of God and a sinful world, between the age to come and the present evil age. The church has experienced the victory of the Kingdom of God;

> and yet the church is, like other men, at the mercy of the powers of this world...
>
> "This very situation creates a severe tension - indeed, acute conflict; for the church is the focal point of the conflict between good and evil, God and Satan, until the end of the age.
>
> "The church can never be at rest or take her ease but must always be the church in struggle and conflict, often persecuted, but sure of the ultimate victory."[3]

The Elder straightened in his chair, removing his glasses with a vigorous motion, eager to make his point. "This is part of the 'already and not yet' dynamic that Ladd has taught us. The apostle John wrote that 'the reason Jesus appeared was to destroy the devil's work'[4], and as long as His followers – we who are the Church universal – remain *in history*, we will find ourselves in the same spiritual conflict with the devil, and with our own sinful nature."

As he spoke, he tapped the little bottle of *salsa picante* with his forefinger, drawing our attention to that symbol of 'the God who comes' within history.

The Elder leaned back in his seat, looking back and forth between us. "That is the 'already' dynamic. The second quote points us towards the 'not yet': the Church will always be at odds with the dominant cultural values that oppose God, and at times will be persecuted for it."

Picking up the pickle fork for emphasis, he added with confidence, "But we can have hope in the ultimate, eventual victory of the Kingdom of God breaking into history, with the return of the King."

The Elder paused, shoulders slumping slightly as the burst of energy left him. "I would like to suggest that the implications of recognizing daily that we are in a spiritual battle would revolutionize how we view the world around us. At the very least, the recognition of our identity as 'resident aliens' should serve as a catalyst to 'keep in step with the Spirit'."[5]

There was a moment of silence at our table – quite uncharacteristic for us – as we each chewed on the morsels the Elder had just shared. The Younger stirred first, drawing our attention with a quiet clearing of his throat.

"To continue on that train of thought," he began, moving his coffee mug out of reach as a precaution, "I was amazed at how many New Testament scriptures fit the 'kingdoms in conflict' worldview, once I was aware of it."

Shifting in his chair as his natural restlessness re-asserted itself, the Younger gestured with his e-reader as he continued to explain.

"For example, you can see 'kingdoms in conflict' in all four Gospels, as well as in Acts. It's probably the most obvious in the Gospel of Mark, where it seems Jesus is casting demons out constantly. Even some of the physical healings that are recorded, although not all, are attributed to demonic interference."

"I noticed the same thing in the Gospel of Luke," I added, pulling out my own Bible. "When Jesus commissioned His disciples, twice, to preach the Kingdom, He specifically included authority to heal disease and cast out demons. Jesus did it first with the twelve disciples[6], and later with seventy-two[7]. If this applies to Jesus' disciples today – meaning, *us* – then we can and should expect to see people healed and demons cast out, as well."

The Younger shifted in his chair, unease adding to his natural tendency to fidget. "And that is where I get uncomfortable, honestly," he admitted candidly, "but not from a theological point of view. I've seen a lot of damage done by people who promised healing, but when nothing happened, they pinned the blame on the sick person."

"There were a great number of people in Jesus' day who weren't healed, either," interjected the Elder gently, his tone one of compassion. "And I'm not just referring to Jesus in His hometown, where He did few miracles because of their lack of faith[8]. I'm thinking of the cripple beside the pool near the Sheep Gate: Jesus walked into a place that was absolutely *filled* with sick people, and yet He healed only one of them[9]. Lazarus was raised from the dead[10], but Jesus' own cousin, John the Baptist, wasn't."[11]

"It's probably the seeming randomness of who receives healing, and who doesn't, that is the most difficult part to understand," I suggested, modeling my tone and body language to match the pastoral example of the Elder. "But I think that the 'already/not yet' of the Kingdom speaks to this, as well."

Now I had the full attention of both the Younger and the Elder. "Ladd explained it this way:

> "Multitudes of deformed, sick, diseased, and dead men in Palestine were untouched by the life of the Kingdom of God. These signs of the Kingdom were only a token, not the fullness of the consummation...
>
> "Here is the mysterious fact about the Kingdom. Its blessings have entered the old age, introducing a new order of life which nevertheless does not bring the old order to its end for all men. The new order is not the age to come, the Eschaton, but is a new order hidden in the old age."[12]

Replacing my book on the table, I attempted to summarize. "Whenever somebody is healed, it's the 'already' of the Kingdom breaking into history. And, sadly, the 'not yet' of the Kingdom is the reason why not everyone is healed."

The Elder looked pensive; I was as aware of his wife's passing as he was of my own infant son's death, some years earlier.

The Younger was privy to those details in both of our lives, and his respectful silence was born from his recognition that neither the Elder nor I were speaking theoretically, but out of our own painful histories.

The Elder roused himself from his thoughts first. "And as far as *praying* for the sick and those afflicted by demonic spirits," he suggested, removing his glasses and briefly pinching the bridge of his nose, "without being trite by any means, may I quote hockey's 'Great One'?"

That brought a measure of relief from the heaviness that had briefly settled over our table, as the Younger and I began to laugh at the inside joke; we knew where the Elder was going. No matter how much teasing he had to endure about his favorite team never making the playoffs, the Elder was a dedicated and tenacious hockey fan.

The Elder smiled with a long-suffering shake of his head. "Indulge me, please, my young friends. Wayne Gretsky, the 'Great One', has been quoted as saying: 'You miss one hundred percent of the shots you never take'. I would like to suggest that the reason we pray for the sick is simply because Jesus instructed us to. The results, however, we must leave to Him."

"I keep going back to when Ladd called healing and deliverance from demons 'tokens', or signs, of the presence of the Kingdom," I chimed in, referring again to my own hand-written notes. "The number of inexplicable, miraculous things done by Jesus, that are recorded in the Gospels, is pretty impressive. And after Pentecost, the disciples saw the same 'tokens' of the Kingdom as they spread the gospel." *(See Appendix: Miracles in Gospels/Acts)*

The Younger opened his mouth as if he was about to speak, but apparently thought better of it, and drank more of his latte instead. The Elder seemed to anticipate the Younger's unspoken objection, and he reached across the table to touch the cuff of his friend's sleeve.

"I believe there is little doubt that healing and deliverance from evil spirits is included in the remarkable impact of the Gospel of the Kingdom," he said kindly but firmly. “But I also share your concerns about the negative impact, in this day and age, that has resulted from the hype and hysteria among many charismatics. And I say that with love and respect, remembering many good friends that we all have in common.”

He sighed, looking briefly in my direction, before turning his attention again to the Younger. “Frankly, it would be much easier to simply avoid anything remotely miraculous, to escape being labeled a ‘charismaniac’. But to be spiritually and intellectually honest, Scripture does not allow us that option. The Holy Spirit of Jesus will continue to work just as He wills, including in the areas of spiritual gifts and the miraculous.

“And therefore, we must continue to embrace the messy task of discernment and -- where appropriate -- warning, teaching and correcting.”

The Younger grimaced, acknowledging with a nod the uncomfortable truth in the Elder’s words. “And we all know how popular it is to speak up about truth and error these days,” he said, unable to prevent a hint of sarcasm from creeping into his voice.

The Younger held up his hands in mock surrender, as he hastened to add, “I know, I know – I’ve read all the warnings in the Old Testament about false prophets[13], and also Jesus’ teaching[14], not to mention Peter[15], John[16], and Paul[17]. I know that we have to beware of the impact of false teaching and false teachers. I just get tired of being labeled ‘judgmental’ and told that I’m arrogant for speaking up.”

The Elder leaned back in his chair, eyes fixed on the exposed metal rafters and light fixtures above us. "Ah, but there is a world of difference between speaking up and being *arrogant*," he sighed heavily. "Pride and arrogance are attitudes of the heart, which overflow into our words and actions.[18]

"It's possible to ask questions that challenge the status quo in either an arrogant or a humble manner, of course," the Elder conceded thoughtfully, shaking his head. "But I find it profoundly disturbing when someone who asks a discerning question is dismissed as arrogant."

He relaxed in his chair, looking to each of us with a slight smile. "I'm sorry. Pet peeve of mine."

"Getting back to the 'tokens' of the Kingdom," I prompted, not willing to lose our thread of conversation, "would it be fair to say that we have to live in the tension between praying for people in faith, and leaving the results to God? Or is that too simplistic?"

The Younger frowned in thought before replying. "To answer your question with another question," he countered, "didn't you just repeat, in different words, what we've already said about the already-and-not-yet Kingdom?"

I could see his point immediately. "Allow me to clarify, then," I suggested with a smile, thankful for the back-and-forth dialogue. "I was remembering your earlier comments about the Kingdom requiring a response from us; that passivity wasn't an option. I was wondering if the tension is a result of us being proactive in praying for people who are sick, even though we know that the 'not yet' might mean the person won't be healed. At least, not healed in this lifetime."

The Younger was ready for that one, as well. "That may be reassuring for the people doing the praying," he pointed out, "but it's cold comfort for the person who doesn't get healed. I'm not trying to argue against what you're saying, I'm only concerned about what this means from the perspective of the sick person."

The Elder interrupted, at his fatherly best once again. "Obedience is the key," he said softly, but with a subtle authority. "The Kingdom is all about the Rule and Reign of God. We come under Jesus' authority when we enter the 'already' of the Kingdom, and at the risk of sounding authoritarian, He *is* the King, after all.

"The discussion you are getting sidetracked into will result in what some would call 'the paralysis of analysis'." He paused briefly as the Younger and I chuckled at his choice of phrase, knowing the high value the Elder placed on the study of theology.

"The questions you are debating are important," the Elder leaned closer as he pressed home his point, "but *only if they do not distract you from actually* ***doing*** *what the Scriptures tell us.*

"Praying for the sick, feeding the hungry, seeking justice for the oppressed, preaching the good news to the poor, that sort of thing. That's what faith is for. Don't talk yourselves out of simple obedience."

The Younger and I exchanged looks, recognizing the wisdom of the Elder's words. "Okay, you've got me," agreed the Younger, suddenly smiling. "I guess I'd rather be the son who tells his Father, 'yes, I will', and then actually does."

The Elder placed both hands palm-down on the table, his body language and facial expression alike communicating an almost child-like delight. "Would anyone like more coffee?" he offered cheerfully, the abrupt change in topic catching us off-guard. And with that, he was already halfway to the espresso bar before either of us could respond.

The Younger watched as the Barista assisted the Elder with his order, and then brightened as a new thought occurred to him. "Did you give any more thought to the title of the book?" he asked, turning back to me. "Will it be apocalyptic, or pastoral, or what exactly?"

I straightened in my chair, at the same time leaning over to adjust the window blinds as the afternoon sun continued to set, painting the outside street in a warm glow. "Believe it or not, I deliberately didn't spend much time agonizing over what to call it. It happened pretty much as I'd hoped: the title -- and the sub-title -- came along and presented themselves during the writing."

The Younger waited patiently, but not for long. "And...?" he prompted, unable to contain himself.

I leaned back in my chair, spreading my hands to indicate the whole interior of the café. "The title of the book will be *The Genesis Café*, followed by the subtitle *Conversations on the Kingdom*."

The Younger nodded in approval, gesturing at the array of books that littered our table. "Well, that's nothing like what I suggested back in the day, but you're right. It fits."

The Elder returned, gingerly holding three coffee mugs by their ceramic handles, trying not to burn himself and offering no explanation for the absence of a tray. Cautiously and with exaggerated reverence, he placed a steaming mug in front of each of us, as the Younger informed him of my proposed name for the book.

"A descriptively accurate title, certainly," he agreed, easing himself past the Younger as he returned to his chair beside the window. "And much less likely to confuse people as to your intent." Without being specific, his meaning was made clear by his exaggerated pantomime of elbowing the Younger in the ribs.

"So, this is it?" asked the Younger, looking slightly disappointed. "I feel like we've only barely begun to scratch the surface."

The Elder tugged not-so-subtly at his copy of Ladd, catching my eye across the table. "Any last thoughts?" I asked innocently, pretending that I hadn't seen the Elder's physical cue. "Comments? Quotations? Confessions?"

"Well, since you asked," began the Elder brightly, bringing his copy of Ladd to our attention with a flourish, "I do have one last comment to make on the already-and-not-yet Kingdom."

With Ladd held aloft in one hand, the Elder paused momentarily as with his other hand, he placed the *salsa picante*, the hamburger-shaped saltshaker, and the inoffensive little pickle fork in a line across the middle of the table.

Turning again to his book, he solemnly intoned, "Will you turn with me, please, in *Jesus and the Kingdom*, to page three hundred and..."

The Younger rolled his eyes, leaning over to bring his e-reader to the attention of the Elder as he interrupted. "What are the chances, *professor*, of your ancient tome and my digital copy having the same page numbers?" he asked, unable to resist the opportunity to respond to the Elder's earlier elbow in the ribs. "I can probably come pretty close, but it's not as exact as you'd think."

The Elder looked in consternation from the Younger to me. "I've got the 1974 paperback version of *The Presence of the Future*," I reminded him, pointing to my copy, "and you've got an original hard cover copy of *Jesus and the Kingdom* from the 1960s, so..." I ended with shrug.

The Elder, unfazed, hardly missed a beat. "Well then, *students,* listen carefully," he cheerfully instructed, his gaze and attention returning to his copy of Ladd.

> **"The tension found in Jesus' teaching between a sense of imminence and a sense of history is, we believe, the tension God purposes for his church. Since the prophetic note of imminence had an ethical orientation, it has an abiding significance. The church should always live with**

> a sense of urgency, feeling the pressure of the end."

> "A dynamic sense of imminence will help the church to preserve its eschatological character and not become absorbed by the world... Sometimes the church forgets its character as an eschatological community that is essentially alien to this age."[19]

The Elder peered at us over the rim of his reading glasses, looking very much the part of a professor. His right hand moved to the three items he'd placed on the table as symbols, touching each in succession as he drew our attention to them.

"The Kingdom is already breaking into history; the 'God who comes' continues to come," he began, his right hand resting first on the *salsa picante*, and then moving to touch the handle of the Pickle Fork of the Apocalypse. "And yet, we dare not become lazy or complacent, because we know that the Kingdom will come in its fullness – the 'big bang' of apocalyptic thought – at any moment. And what Ladd refers to as *imminence* is just this: we simply don't know how much time is left to be about the mission of Jesus."

His hand finally came to rest on the saltshaker. "Because we have been touched by the Kingdom, and we live in expectation of the Kingdom coming, we are called to 'produce fruit in keeping with repentance'. The Sermon on the Mount, many of the Parables, and a great deal found in the Epistles, all speak to this. Our ethical behavior, including our involvement in the issues of justice, are just a few of the facets of living under the Rule and Reign of Jesus in His Kingdom."

He read again from his copy of Ladd, still held aloft in his left hand.

> "However, a sense of history is also necessary to guard against fanaticism, date-setting and short-sightedness. A consciousness of this tension between history and eschatology would give to every generation of believers a powerful motivation and dynamic.
>
> "The realization that they may well be the last generation before the final victory of the Kingdom, and yet the necessity to plan and work with the sanity of a long perspective for the future is a biblical tension."[20]

"We don't bring the Kingdom," I said, recalling our earlier discussions. "Only Jesus brings the Kingdom, and we are invited to participate with Him in His story."

The Younger sipped his coffee, collecting his thoughts. "I was looking forward to studying Ladd because I wanted to understand what Jesus meant by 'the Kingdom is near' in His day," he said slowly, setting his mug down again. "But the take-away that means the most, even though I know it will be uncomfortable at times, is a deeper understanding of the ongoing *mission* of Jesus, and my part in it."

"And the forceful ones lay hold of it," concurred the Elder, quietly.

I closed my denim journal with a sense of finality, noticing the early evening crowd beginning to trickle into the café as the sunlight outside gave way to the cooler blanket of dusk.

In another telling sign, the Barista was no longer visible behind the espresso bar; her shift must have ended shortly after helping the Elder with our latest round of caffeine.

The Elder followed my lead, beginning to pack his kitchen metaphors and books into his weathered satchel as a prelude to concluding our time together.

"This calls for a toast," exclaimed the Younger enthusiastically, as he shut down his e-reader and stowed it in his messenger bag. And with that announcement, he stood to his feet, lifting his half-empty (or was it half-full?) coffee mug over the middle of the table.

There was a scraping of chairs on the floor, as the Elder and I also stood, raising our coffee mugs to match the Younger's. Then came a sudden and unexpectedly awkward pause, as each of us looked to the other, unsure how we should proceed.

"What should we toast to?" I asked, momentarily stymied, as I looked back and forth at my two friends.

The Younger frowned wordlessly as he shook his head, equally at a loss. Perhaps not surprisingly, it was the Elder who broke the silence.

"To the King and His Kingdom," he suggested, quietly but with great conviction.

A wide grin spread across the Younger's face as he nodded, and I knew the Elder had, once again, found just the right words for the moment. Our mugs clinked exuberantly together, the sharp sound ringing out in the café, as we unreservedly echoed the Elder's words.

"To the King and His Kingdom!"

Coffee & Toast Notes

1. *The Presence of the Future*, 137
2. Ibid., 303
3. Ibid., 338
4. 1 John 3:7
5. Galatians 5:16-26
6. Mark 6:7-13, Luke 9:1-6
7. Luke 10:1-17
8. Matthew 13:54-58; Mark 6:4-6
9. John 5:2-14
10. John 11:38-44
11. Matthew 14:6-12; Mark 6:17-29
12. *The Presence of the Future*, 204
13. For example: Jeremiah 23:9-40; Ezekiel 13:1-23
14. Matthew 7:15-23
15. 2 Peter 2:1-22
16. 1 John 4:1; Revelation 2:2
17. Acts 20:28-31; 2 Corinthians 11:3-5, 13-15; 1 Timothy 1:3-11; 2 Timothy 4:1-5
18. Luke 6:43-45
19. *The Presence of the Future,* 338-339
20. Ibid., 339

Further Conversations

1. Where do you see the possiblity of 'tension' between the values of the world (in your context) and the values of the Kingdom?

2. There is an old saying: "If the Holy Spirit was removed from the earth today, 90% of church activity would continue without even noticing." Okay, a little cynical but not without some truth. But let's not let ourselves off the hook: if the Holy Spirit was removed from the earth today, would ***we*** notice, and if so, in what areas of our lives?

3. It has been said: "Faith is spelled R-I-S-K." Praying for the sick and the demonized would qualify as a risk for most of us. Would you be more comfortable (a) serving the poor at a shelter or (b) praying for someone else's release from demonic attack? Which requires risk/faith for you? Where are you 'playing it safe'?

4. Brainstorm together:

   (a) Which aspect of the already-and-not-yet Kingdom was the most unexpected?

   (b) What does 'produce the fruit of repentance' look like for you? (Ie. What areas have you been most challenged in?)

   (c) What risks have you felt God is prodding you to take? Can you take them together (safety and encouragement in groups)? When?

<u>Extra Credit</u>

1. Look through the Appendix: *Miracles in Gospels/Acts* together. How do we live in a biblical tension between expecting/praying to see the Spirit move in power, without becoming obsessed and/or side-tracked by seeking miracles?
2. "The meat is in the street." Discuss this statement in light of the previous question.

about the author

Robby McAlpine is just a regular guy who loves to write. And play bass. Sure, he has a couple of theological degrees, but in reality, there are just a few things he's truly passionate about: discipleship, passing the torch to the next generation, and authentic community (usually involving lots of laughter and good coffee).

Robby's other books include *Detoxing from Church,* and *Post-Charismatic 2.0: Rekindle the Smoldering Wick.*

He lives with his family in British Columbia, Canada.

Robby has been blogging since 2003 at *www.robbymcalpine.com.* Drop by for a visit! (B.Y.O.Coffee)

Other books by Robby McAlpine:

Detoxing from Church

Jesus is building His church, and the gates of hell are no match for it. So why are so many of His followers tired, disillusioned, and ready to give up on the church?

Mixing humor, modern parables, and personal insights gleaned via the School of Hard Knocks, *Detoxing from Church* is a redemptive look at the process of recovery from wounds and disillusionment, and finding our identity anew in Jesus.

Detoxing from Church is a journey, and it is also an invitation:

Jesus is still building His church.

Available at Amazon

POST-CHARISMATIC 2.0:
REKINDLE THE SMOLDERING WICK

"I don't want to be post-Spirit, but I wouldn't mind being post-*hype*."

Post-charismatics are caught between a rock and a hard place: They believe that the gifts of the Holy Spirit are for today. But they have also seen the twisted teachings and spiritual abuses that exist in the charismatic movement.

And so the sifting process must begin.

* * *

Robby McAlpine writes with a positive and constructive voice. He shows us that the answer to misuse or excess concerning the Holy Spirit is not 'no use' but right use.

For burned-out and hurt former charismatics, *Post-Charismatic* leads the way forward toward a mature and sane re-engagement with the person and work of the Holy Spirit. *Post-Charismatic* is not post-Holy Spirit, it is a call for post-weirdness.

Bishop Todd D. Hunter
Anglican Church in North America

I not only like what McAlpine has to say; I like the spirit in which he says it. Highly recommended.

Brian Kerr
FM Bookshop.com (UK)

I first started this book when the whole *Strange Fire* controversy was in full swing, and I remember thinking, "this book is the anti-strange fire". McAlpine offers an honest critique of the imbalances of the Charismatic movements, but he never uses those imbalances as a spear to impale the notion of the continuation of the gifts of the Holy Spirit. I found the writing style to be incredibly honest, but incredibly gracious and emotionally mature.

Kenny Burchard
ThinkTheology.org

I have read both the first and second editions of this book and I can't express how impressed I am with Rob's balanced and fair treatment of the issues. A must read!

Mike Horn
The River Church, Fresno CA

Available at Amazon

appendix 1: jesus' teaching on separation

The following list includes verses in which Jesus spoke explicitly about the separation dynamic of the Kingdom, as well as verses in which Jesus warned of the reality of hell (implied separation).

Matthew	**Mark**	**Luke**	**John**
3:10-12	9:42-48	3:7-18	3:16-18
5:22	10:17-25	6:46-49	3:34-36
5:29-30	12:1-9	8:16-18	5:24-30
7:13-14	13:16-17	10:8-12	6:53-69
7:16-20	16:15-16	10:13-15	9:35-41
7:21-23		12:1-10	12:44-50
8:11-12		12:42-46	20:19-23
10:28		13:23-28	
10:32-33		14:15-24	
11:20-24		16:19-31	
13:24-30		19:11-26	
13:36-43		20:9-19	
13:47-50			
18:8-9			
21:43			
22:1-14			
23:15			
23:33			
24:30-31			
24:38-41			
24:45-51			
25:1-13			
25:14-29			
25:31-46			

appendix 2: gospel of the kingdom in acts

Acts	Speaker	Listeners	Summary
2:14-21	Peter	Jews (many nations)	• Jesus is the Messiah • You killed Him • Resurrection (God's vindication) • Repent & be baptized • Forgiveness of sins • Receive gift of the Holy Spirit
3:11-26	Peter	Jews (in Temple)	• Jesus is the Messiah • You killed Him • Resurrection (God's vindication) • Repent & turn to God • Forgiveness of sins
4:5-12	Peter	Jewish religious leaders	• Jesus is the Messiah ('Christ' is Greek translation) • You killed Him • Resurrection (God's vindication) • Jesus the only way to salvation
5:27-32	Peter	Sanhedrin	• Jesus is the Savior & Prince @ God's right hand • You killed Him • Resurrection (God's vindication) • Repentance & forgiveness of sins

Acts	Speaker	Listeners	Summary
7:1-60	Stephen	Sanhedrin	• Abraham given the Covenant • Moses brought deliverance from Egyptian captivity • "God will send a prophet like me" (same words by Peter in Acts 3:11-26) • People rejected God to worship Golden Calf • People rejected God to worship false gods (leading to Babylonian exile) • You are the same: you killed the Messiah • Resurrection (saw Jesus standing @ the right hand of the Father)
10:34-48	Peter	Gentiles	• Jesus is the Messiah • He was killed by His own people • Resurrection (God's vindication) • Forgiveness of sins • Gift of the Holy Spirit • Baptized after the fact

Acts	Speaker	Listeners	Summary
13:15-41	Paul	Local synagogue in Pisidian Antioch	Israel History Lesson: • Exodus from Egypt • First judges given by God, later people chose a king (Saul), later replaced by David • Jesus is descended from David, and is the Savior • He was killed by His own people • Resurrection (God's vindication) – very similar wording to Peter @ Pentecost in Acts 2) • Forgiveness of sins
17:1-4	Paul	Local synagogue in Thessalonica	• Spent time "proving" from the Scriptures (Old Testament) that the Messiah would suffer & die, and then the Resurrection • Jesus is the promised Messiah
17:16-32	Paul	Gentile philosophers in Athens	• One God who created all nations • He has appointed a day to judge the world with justice • He has appointed a judge: the one resurrected from the dead

Acts	Speaker	Listeners	Summary
26:1-29	Paul	King Agrippa's Court	• Jesus is the Messiah (fulfillment of the Abrahamic Covenant) • Forgiveness of sins • Turning people from darkness to light; from Satan's power to God's • Repent & produce fruit of repentance • Jesus suffered and was resurrected; a light to His people and Gentiles alike

appendix 3: miracles in gospels/acts

Where	Who	What
Matthew 1:18	Mary	Pregnant "through the Holy Spirit"
Matthew 1:19-24	Joseph	Angelic messenger in a dream
Matthew 2:13, 19-20, 22-23	Joseph	Angelic messengers (3 instances) in his dreams; fulfilling prophecy
Matthew 3:16-17	Jesus	Spirit descending like a dove, voice of the Father audibly heard
Matthew 4:23-24	Jesus	Healing many types of disease Cast out demons
Matthew 8:1-4	Jesus	Healed a man with leprosy
Matthew 8:5-13	Jesus	Healed the centurion's servant from a distance; praised centurion's faith
Matthew 8:14-15	Jesus	Healed Peter's mother of a fever
Matthew 8:16-17	Jesus	Cast out many demons
Matthew 8:23-27	Jesus	Rebukes a storm
Matthew 8:28-34	Jesus	Cast out demons (two men)
Matthew 9:1-8	Jesus	Healed a paralytic
Matthew 9:18-26	Jesus	Healed a woman "subject to bleeding" Raised a young girl from the dead
Matthew 9:27-31	Jesus	Healed two blind men

Where	Who	What
Matthew 9:32-33	Jesus	Healed a mute man by casting out a demon
Matthew 9:35	Jesus	Went to numerous towns preaching the Kingdom and healing every kind of disease
Matthew 10:1-11	Jesus, the 12 disciples	Jesus commissions the disciples to "preach the Kingdom is near", heal the sick, cast out demons
Matthew 12:9-13	Jesus	Healed a man with a withered hand
Matthew 12:15	Jesus	Healed many from every kind of disease
Matthew 12:22-23	Jesus	Healed a deaf-mute by casting out a demon
Matthew 13:58	Jesus	Could not do many miracles due to lack of faith in His hometown
Matthew 14:14	Jesus	Healed many in a crowd
Matthew 14:15-21	Jesus, 12 disciples	Multiplies food for five thousand people
Matthew 14:22-32	Jesus	Walks on the water; Peter as well
Matthew 14:35-36	Jesus	All who were brought to Him were healed
Matthew 15:21-28	Jesus	Healed a Canaanite woman's daughter at a distance from demonic
Matthew 15:30-31	Jesus	Lame, blind, crippled, mute and "many others" all healed
Matthew 15:32-38	Jesus, 12 disciples	Multiplies food for four thousand people

Where	Who	What
Matthew 17:1-8	Jesus, Peter, James, John	Transfiguration of Jesus
Matthew 17:14-18	Jesus	Healed a boy of seizures by casting out a demon
Matthew 19:1-2	Jesus	Large crowds healed
Matthew 21:12-14	Jesus	Cleared the temple; blind and lame healed
Matthew 21:18-19	Jesus	Fig tree is cursed due to lack of fruit
Matthew 27:51-53	Many deceased "holy people"	Raised from the dead when Jesus died Temple curtain torn in two
Matthew 28:2-4	Angel, Roman guards	Violent earthquake as angel comes to remove the stone from Jesus' tomb
Mark 1:9-11	Jesus	Holy Spirit descends at Jesus' baptism like a dove; the Father audibly speaks
Mark 1:21-28	Jesus	Cast out a demon during a synagogue service in Capernaum
Mark 1:29-31	Jesus	Healed Peter's mother of a fever
Mark 1:32-34	Jesus	Healed disease and cast out demons
Mark 1:40-42	Jesus	Healed a man of leprosy
Mark 2:1-12	Jesus	Healed a paralytic (lowered through the roof by his friends)
Mark 3:1-5	Jesus	Healed a man with a shriveled hand
Mark 3:7-12	Jesus	"Healed many", and cast out demons
Mark 4:35-41	Jesus	Calms the storm

Where	Who	What
Mark 5:2-15	Jesus	Cast out a "legion" of demons from a single man – 2000 pigs drowned as a result
Mark 5:22-42	Jesus	Healed a woman "subject to bleeding" Raised Jairus' daughter from the dead
Mark 6:4-6	Jesus	Healed a "few"; amazed at lack of faith in His hometown
Mark 6:7-13	Jesus, 12 disciples	Gave the disciples authority over evil spirits; they preached repentance, cast out demons and healed the sick
Mark 6:34-44	Jesus, 12 disciples	Multiplied food for five thousand people
Mark 6:45-52	Jesus	Jesus walks on water, calms the storm
Mark 6:54-56	Jesus	Healed many people of many diseases, in many locations
Mark 7:24-30	Jesus	Cast a demon out of a Greek woman's daughter at a distance
Mark 7:31-37	Jesus	Healed a deaf-mute by casting out a demon
Mark 8:1-18	Jesus, 12 disciples	Multiplied food for four thousand people
Mark 8:22-25	Jesus	Healed a blind man
Mark 9:2-8	Jesus, Peter, James, John	Transfiguration of Jesus
Mark 9:17-27	Jesus	Cast demon out of a mute boy who also had seizures; "healed" by having demon cast out

Where	Who	What
Mark 10:46-52	Jesus	Healed Bartimaeus of blindness
Mark 15:37-39	Jesus	Temple curtain torn in two as Jesus died
Mark 16:2-7	Mary, Mary Magdalene, Salome	"Young man in white" (angel?) inside tomb announced that Jesus had risen (and who moved the stone?)
Luke 1:11-22	Zechariah	Gabriel (angel) appears to prophesy the birth of John the Baptist; strikes Zechariah mute until birth as a sign
Luke 1:26-38	Mary	Gabriel (angel) appears to prophesy the birth of Jesus
Luke 2:8-15	Shepherds	Group of angels announce birth of Jesus
Luke 2:25-35	Simeon	Holy Spirit had told him that he would see the Messiah before he died Prophesied to Mary & Joseph about the newborn Jesus
Luke 3:21-22	Jesus	Spirit descends like a dove during baptism of Jesus; the Father speaks audibly
Luke 4:31-37	Jesus	Cast out a demon during a synagogue service in Capernaum
Luke 4:38-39	Jesus	Healed Peter's mother of a fever
Luke 4:40-41	Jesus	Healed many diseases and cast out demons
Luke 5:1-11	Jesus	Miraculous catch of fish; results in Peter, James & John becoming first disciples
Luke 5:12-15	Jesus	Healed a man of leprosy

Where	Who	What
Luke 5:17-26	Jesus	Healing many Healed paralytic (lowered through roof by his friends)
Luke 6:6-19	Jesus	Healed a man with a shriveled hand
Luke 6:17-19	Jesus	Healing all who came to him; cast out many demons
Luke 7:2-10	Jesus	Healed centurion's servant at a distance; praised centurion's faith
Luke 7:12-17	Jesus	Raised a widow's son from death
Luke 7:20-22	Jesus	Healing many when John the Baptist's disciples asked if He was truly the Messiah Jesus' "proof" included the sick being healed
Luke 8:1-2	Jesus	Travelling with "some women" who had been healed of disease and evil spirits, including Mary Magdalene
Luke 8:22-25	Jesus	Calms the storm
Luke 8:26-39	Jesus	Cast out a "legion" of demons The man returned to his home town and spread the news of Jesus everywhere
Luke 8:40-55	Jesus	Healed a woman "subject to bleeding" Raised Jairus' daughter from the dead
Luke 9:1-6	Jesus, 12 disciples	Commissioned to preach, heal the sick, cast out demons Disciples "healed people everywhere"

Where	Who	What
Luke 9:12-17	Jesus, 12 disciples	Multiplied food for five thousand people
Luke 9:28-36	Jesus, Peter, James, John	Transfiguration of Jesus
Luke 9:10-11	Jesus	Taught the Kingdom of God, healed the sick
Luke 9:38-43	Jesus	Cast a demon out of a boy that was causing him convulsions; "healed" the boy of the demon
Luke 10:1-20	Jesus, 72 disciples	Commissioned to preach the Kingdom and heal the sick Returned to say that demons "submitted" at the name of Jesus
Luke 11:14	Jesus	Cast out a demon that made a boy mute
Luke 13:10-13	Jesus	Cast a demon out of a woman who had been crippled by the demon (bent over)
Luke 14:1-6	Jesus	Healed a man of "dropsy"
Luke 17:11-19	Jesus	Healed ten men of leprosy; only the Samaritan returned to give thanks
Luke 18:35-43	Jesus	Healed a blind man just outside Jericho
Luke 22:49-51	Jesus	Healed an ear cut off by an over-zealous disciple during the arrest of Jesus
Luke 23:44-46	Jesus	Temple curtain torn in two as Jesus died
Luke 24:1-8	The women	Two "men in white" (angels?) at the tomb announced that Jesus is risen

Where	Who	What
Luke 24:13-32	Emmaus Road disciples, Jesus	Jesus appeared in disguised form, discussed how the O.T.; when the disciples recognize Him, He disappeared
John 1:32-34	John the Baptist	Holy Spirit told him that Jesus was the Messiah; saw the Spirit descend on Him during Jesus' baptism
John 2:1-11	Jesus	Turned water into wine at a wedding in Cana
John 4:45-54	Jesus	Healed a royal official's son at a distance
John 5:2-14	Jesus	Healed a cripple by a pool by the Sheep Gate in Jerusalem
John 6:1-15	Jesus	Multiplied food for five thousand people
John 6:16-21	Jesus	Jesus walks on water
John 9:1-7	Jesus	Healed a blind man by making mud with His spit, and telling him to wash in the Pool of Siloam
John 11:38-44	Jesus	Raised Lazarus from the dead, four days later
John 12:23-31	Jesus	The Father speaks audibly from heaven in answer to Jesus
John 20:19-20	Jesus	Suddenly appeared among the disciples while they were behind locked doors
John 20:26-27	Jesus	Sudden appearance #2: again, doors were locked
John 20:30	Jesus	Many other miracles not recorded; the ones that were recorded were to back up claim that Jesus is the Messiah

miracles in gospels/acts

Where	Who	What
John 21:2-7	Jesus	Miraculous catch of fish
Acts 2:1-21	"All together" (possibly as many as 120)	Sound like a mighty wind; tongues of fire on each disciple; all were filled with the Holy Spirit and spoke in tongues (known languages, at least 15 mentioned) 3000 put their faith in Jesus
Acts 2:42-44	Apostles	Many "signs and miraculous wonders" New believers on a daily basis
Acts 3:1-10	Peter & John	Healed a cripple by the temple gate; the cripple was then able to enter the temple Many put their faith in Jesus
Acts 4:23-31	Peter, John, unspecified number of disciples	Building was shaken after they prayed for more power to be bold with the gospel of the Kingdom (in view of threats from religious leaders)
Acts 5:12-16	Peter & the apostles	Many "miraculous signs and wonders", many healed of disease (even by Peter's shadow), many demons cast out Many put their faith in Jesus
Acts 5:17-20	Unidentified apostles	Angel releases them from prison after religious leaders arrested them
Acts 6:8	Stephen	"Great wonders and miraculous signs"
Acts 7:55-56	Stephen	Saw a vision of Jesus at the right hand of God

Where	Who	What
Acts 8:4-8	Philip	Many "miraculous signs", healed many paralytics and cripples, many demons cast out Many put their faith in Jesus
Acts 8:14-17	Peter & John	Prayed that the Samaritan believers would receive the Holy Spirit Whatever happened is not recorded, but it was noteworthy enough that Simon the Magician offered money for the ability
Acts 8:36-40	Philip	"Taken away" by the Spirit after baptizing the Ethiopian eunuch; "appeared" in town of Azotus
Acts 9:1-9	Saul the Pharisee	Trip to persecute Christians was high-jacked by a vision of Jesus; Saul is blinded by the encounter
Acts 9:10-16	Ananias	Had a vision that he was to go and pray for Saul the Pharisee
Acts 9:17-19	Ananias	Healed Saul's blindness in Jesus' name
Acts 9:32-35	Peter	Healed Aeneas of blindness "all" of Lydda and Sharon put their faith in Jesus
Acts 9:36-42	Peter	Raised Tabitha from the dead Many in Joppa put their faith in Jesus
Acts 10:9-19	Peter	Vision of the sheet filled with "unclean" animals; Holy Spirit tells Peter to go to Cornelius' place (a Gentile)

Where	Who	What
Acts 10:44-48	Peter, Jewish disciples, Gentile believers	Holy Spirit is poured out on the Gentiles Speaking in tongues and praising God
Acts 11:27-30	Agabus	One of the prophets from Jerusalem, predicted "through the Spirit" a famine
Acts 12:1-17	Peter	Angel releases Peter from prison after King Herod arrested him
Acts 13:1-3	Paul & Barnabas	During worship, Holy Spirit directs that they be sent out as missionaries
Acts 13:6-12	Saul/Paul	Paul rebukes a sorcerer, who goes blind for a short while
Acts 14:3	Paul & Barnabas	"Miraculous signs and wonders" in Iconium, where they spent "considerable time" preaching about Jesus
Acts 14:8-10	Paul & Barnabas	Healed a man crippled in his feet; crowd tried to sacrifice to them, some Jewish trouble-makers won over the mob, Paul was stoned but survived
Acts 16:6-10	Paul	Spirit of Jesus prevented them from Bithynia Paul has a vision redirecting them to Macedonia
Acts 16:16-18	Paul & Silas	Cast out a demon from a fortune-telling girl
Acts 16:22-34	Paul & Silas	Miraculously freed from prison Jailor & entire family put their faith in Jesus

Where	Who	What
Acts 18:9-11	Paul	Vision from God to encourage Paul to continue preaching the gospel of the Kingdom
Acts 19:1-6	Paul, 12 Ephesian disciples	Paul baptizes the believers in the name of Jesus, and the Holy Spirit "came on them" Speaking in tongues and prophesying
Acts 19:11-12	Paul	"Extraordinary miracles", including healing many and casting out many demons Many put their faith in Jesus (This took place during an extended ministry tour of two years in Ephesus)
Acts 20:7-12	Paul	Raised Eutychus from the dead after he fell asleep during Paul's extremely long sermon
Acts 21:8-11	Paul, Philip, & Agabus	Philip had four daughters who prophesied Agabus prophesied of Paul's arrest
Acts 22:11	Paul	Jesus appears to Paul to encourage him to boldly speak in Rome
Acts 27:21-26	Paul	Angelic messenger in a vision says that Paul & all his traveling companions will survive the storm they were in
Acts 28:3-5	Paul	Suffers a bite from a poisonous viper but shows no ill effects

Where	**Who**	**What**
Acts 28:7-9	Paul	Healed the chief official's father of fever and dysentery "The rest of the island" (of Malta) healed of their diseases

bibliography

George Eldon Ladd

The Presence of the Future: The Eschatology of Biblical Realism; Grand Rapids MI, Wm. B. Eerdmans Publishing Company, 1974 (reprint edition 1996)

Gospel of the Kingdom: Scriptural Studies in the Kingdom of God; Grand Rapids MI, Wm. B. Eerdmans Publishing Company, 1990

> (For those interested in reading Ladd for themselves, I would recommend starting with *Gospel of the Kingdom* as the most accessible -- and perhaps not surprisingly, the shortest -- of Ladd's written works.)

Crucial Questions About the Kingdom of God; Grand Rapids MI, Wm. B. Eerdmans Publishing Company, 1952

A Theology of the New Testament; Grand Rapids MI, Wm. B. Eerdmans Publishing Company, 1974 (revised 1993)

John A. D'Elia

A Place at the Table: George Eldon Ladd and the Rehabilitation of Evangelical Scholarship in America; Oxford, U.K.; Oxford University Press, 2008

57590353R00163

Made in the USA
Lexington, KY
18 November 2016